THE PERILOUS STEP

BY

EILEEN T. FLAHERTY

Published 2020 by King's Bridge, an imprint of Rook Creek LLC

The Perilous Step

Edited by Deanna Sjolander
Cover by Patrick Knowles

Inquiries should be addressed to:
info@rookcreekbooks.com

Publisher's Cataloging-in-Publication Data

Flaherty, Eileen T.
perilous step/ Eileen T. Flaherty; [edited by Deanna Sjolander]. -- 1st ed. --
Chicago, IL : King's Bridge, 2020.
210 p.
ISBN-13 9781948790482: ISBN-10 1948790483

Printed in the United States of America

DEDICATION

This book is dedicated to my family, and I owe everything to them:

Therese – Best Mom

William – Best Dad

Ryan – Best Nephew

Dan – Best Nephew

Shari – Best Sister-in-Law

Kevin – Best Brother

(Bridie Barton – Best Grandma I never knew)

(Tom Barton – Best Grandpa I barely knew)

I didn't write this book for fame or fortune, but because I wanted my nephews to know their grandparents, since they were so young when they passed away, and to know more about the family.

FOREWORD

It is with gratitude that I write this book.

It goes without saying that none of us would be here without our parents. I was a lucky gal to get mine and I would never have picked any others. My mom, Therese Barton, was born to Thomas Barton and Bridie Herlihy. My grandmother, whom sadly I never knew, was one of around fourteen children born in County Kerry, Ireland. On a trip there once, I actually saw the house where she was born and raised. She and most of her siblings immigrated to the United States to find more opportunities because there weren't any in Ireland at the time, except for maybe farming.

You see, I am the granddaughter of immigrant grandparents. My mom was the first generation to be born here. My grandparents came with nothing and stayed with family members until they could get jobs and support themselves. There were no handouts, and they didn't expect any. If you came, you had to make it on your own, and then you were expected to do the same for other relatives, which my grandparents did.

When my grandfather arrived in the United States, he made his way to Chicago and found a job working for an electric company, Commonwealth Edison. Irish immigrants found work in the more dangerous jobs, like as policeman or a fireman and in the electric and gas companies, because you could get hurt or killed, and a lot of people didn't want those types of jobs. Irish immigrants were happy to have them because they wanted to work, save, and make a better life for the next generation.

My grandfather didn't have some cushy office job at Commonwealth Edison; he worked on the streets on power lines. I don't know if either of my grandparents went to or finished high school. They didn't go to college since there was no way for them to do that back then. Nobody had any money for that kind of luxury. You had to work and support yourself at an early age.

After both of my grandparents had come to the United States, they met and got married. I don't know much of that story because my grandmother passed away before I was born, and my grandfather died when I was three and a half. My grandparents had a son whose name was Jack, and I never knew Jack either. When he was about eight or nine, they agreed to let him go back to Ireland with a relative for a trip. He was killed riding a horse, so my grandparents never wanted to go back to their home country of Ireland, and they never did.

A few years later, my mom was born Therese Marie Barton. She would be called Therese. I have heard that she was such a blessing and a joy to them, particularly because of all that they had been through in life. She was an only child. My mom was about twenty when her mother died. She never talked about it much, but I knew that she missed her a lot. During some holidays, Thanksgiving and Christmas, I would see tears in her eyes and ask her what was wrong. She would say, "Oh, nothing," but I would later learn what she must have been thinking and feeling.

As for my dad's parents, I believe that his dad immigrated here from Ireland and that he was from Galway. There were a lot of Flahertys around there.

There used to be a town gate in Galway that said, "From the ferocious O'Flaherty's, Good Lord deliver us!" I like that. On the Flaherty family crest, which is a symbol of Irish heritage, it says in Gaelic, "Fortune Favors the Bold." I love that.

His parents got divorced when my dad was young, which was unheard of at the time, so he, his brother, and sister lived with their father, who died when my dad was in his teens. He was mostly raised by his only sister. I barely knew my grandmother on my dad's side.

I think that when kids are young, they know what their parents do for them, on a surface level. I think the levels and depth of appreciation and gratitude grow as the years go by. Later you think back and realize all that they sacrificed to give you a good life. My parents sure did. They were selfless people.

My mom was a beautiful Irish woman who was stunning and classy, and she had this perfect smile. She had so much elegance and style in everything that she did, and everyone loved my mom. When she walked into a room, everyone stared and wanted to know her. I am not sure, though, whether I inherited all of her characteristics. While I try to be like her, I might take a break from that in some parts of this book.

My mom went to high school and then, when she graduated, she got a job like all of her girlfriends did; the gals didn't go to college. If she had gone to college, she could have been anything—a lawyer, doctor, or even the president because she was smart and had a way with people.

My dad had it a bit harder, as he had lost his father when he was in his teens. He went to high school and then, after graduation, he enlisted in the United States Marine Corps. There were no college opportunities for guys like him in Chicago. They had no money, and he was expected to serve in the military. If he had gone to college, he, too, could have been anything he wanted.

My mom and dad went to different high schools and then met and dated. They wrote letters to each other while my dad was away in the Marines. While he was away, my mom's mother died.

After my dad returned from the service, they got engaged and then married. After the wedding, they got an apartment with my grandfather. It was on the south side of Chicago in a neighborhood that is now considered very dangerous, and I can't go there anymore. In those days, if you had an apartment, you had to buy your own refrigerator. I mention this because, sixty years later, that tangerine-colored monster is still in our basement. Although it doesn't work anymore, I love that refrigerator.

After being married for over a year, in 1956, my parents had their first child Kevin Patrick Flaherty. I can tell from the pictures how happy they must have been to start a family. He was a beautiful baby boy. My dad kept working hard to support them, even working part-time on the weekends delivering pizzas, and my mom stayed at home and made sure that everything was perfect. My grandfather was there to help too.

Then, two years later, in 1958, I was born Eileen Therese Flaherty. I can tell from the pictures that my parents were very happy to have me too, and I had beautiful baby dresses. They were overjoyed to have the perfect family, with one boy and one girl, and that was all they needed. My brother and I have been close throughout the years, and he has been my sideline coach when I had my big jobs with the career knife fights and all, but I will get to those a bit later.

After a few years of my parents being married with two young kids and saving every penny, they were ready to buy a house and got one in an area that was unincorporated and very rural. There were only a few houses on the block where they looked, and the streets were made of coarse stones. I think my grandfather had some influence on the decision, as that is where they picked.

The house was a new construction and it was brick. It had a front room, three bedrooms, a bathroom, a kitchen, and a basement. That was it. They bought that house, and I still have the original sales receipt. The house cost $17,500, and it was the only house we ever had.

Eventually, the unincorporated area became its own city with about thirty thousand people. The streets got paved and there were parks and, eventually, a library and a community pool. My grandfather had been right all along.

I also remember at three years old that I wanted a horse. I asked my mom and, of course, she said no. She wasn't having a horse in the backyard, so I went to ask my grandfather. At an early age, I started to hone my negotiating skills. He adored my brother and me, and I pleaded for the horse and said that I would take care of it. I even had a name picked out for my soon-to-be new horse—Flicka. I dreamed of walking around the backyard with Flicka and that he would be my new best friend. And I wanted Flicka to be red.

My grandfather wanted to give me anything that he could, so he thought I should have the horse. He went to my mom, and she wanted to know where we would keep a horse. Although he thought the backyard would be just fine, my mom was having none of it and said no.

Oh, Flicka, I would always miss the horse I never knew.

We were so lucky to have my grandfather live with us, even if it wasn't for a long time. Although I was young when he died, I still have memories of some of the times we had spent together. He used to take us to a hamburger shop a few blocks away. We walked there, grandfather, my brother, and me, and you felt so important to be with him. He made you feel like he was glad that you were there.

When I was three and a half, my grandfather died unexpectedly, and that was sad, although I was too young to fully appreciate how final that was. He had always been so important in our lives, and how would we go on without him? And now my mom had no parents. I would later sadly learn what that grief is like. She had to be strong and go on because she had two young children. We were too young to think much about it, but later in life, I realized how hard that must have been for her.

As time went by, there were more houses on the block and more kids and neighbors. Some of them are still there, as most of them stayed their whole lives, raised families, and retired there. I knew all of them well and stayed in touch with the neighbors we were close to. Pat and Jim lived across the street, and we were close to them. Maureen and Ben lived a few houses away from them, and we were close to them too. Such great people. Nothing fancy, just hardworking, honest, wonderful family people.

Thanks, Mom and Dad. Miss you both forever and ever.

CHAPTER ONE

I AM ACTUALLY HERE

It is March 25, 2019. I am in Washington, DC, standing on the top step of the United States Supreme Court building with tears in my eyes. Today and tomorrow mark two days in my life that I will never forget—although, most days I have never forgotten, as the Irish can be that way. It is getting dark and I am really cold and should leave, but looking at the Capitol and taking it all in, I don't want to.

I can't move and can't believe that I am here.

Tomorrow I am being sworn into the United States Supreme Court Bar. Me, Eileen T. Flaherty, from Burbank (not California), Illinois, the kid that was never supposed to make it, let alone make it here.

CHAPTER TWO
ST. ALBERT THE GREAT

Where I lived in Burbank, kids didn't go to preschool to learn because the thought was that you shouldn't be sending kids to school too early. Kids were supposed to be kids, and school and responsibilities would come soon enough.

There was one school that offered kindergarten, and you could go there the year before you were supposed to start the first grade. My brother had gone there two years before, and now it was my turn.

The first day was scary, and then it was fine, and it was fun. We didn't learn anything, as it was more socialization to prepare kids for the first grade. There were toys but no books, and each kid had to bring a blanket because we got nap time. It also was only a few days a week, and about two hours, including nap time, because parents at that time didn't want kids to be overburdened. Things have obviously changed, with kids now expected to have read *Moby Dick* and learned algebra before kindergarten.

It was the summer before the first grade, and I was very excited to start my new real school. In my neighborhood, there were two schools that parents could choose from. There was the Catholic school, St. Albert the Great, and the public school, Kennedy. The Catholics sent their kids to the Catholic school, and the publics sent their kids to the public school—there were no charter schools or magnet schools. It was all pretty simple, and nobody had to interview to get into schools or compete for spots.

I was happy to be going to St. Albert the Great. It sounded so important. I felt sorry for the kids who must have been going to some other St. Albert school, as it wasn't the Great one like mine.

In the Catholic schools, kids had to wear uniforms. You had to go to the specific store and buy exactly what was required. For the first graders, the girls had to wear a plaid jumper with an emblem on the right chest that said SAG (for St. Albert the Great) and a white short-sleeved shirt. We had to wear dress shoes, and white socks were a must. The boys had to wear blue pants and a short-sleeved white shirt. They had little clip-on ties, which had the same plaid as the girls' jumpers.

There was no fashion allowed, except for the first few days of school when it was so hot you could wear anything your parents wanted, within reason, because there was no air-conditioning. For the first week, we got to wear our own clothes. I had a few outfits that my mom had gotten for me, and I thought I looked very nice. It was important because I wanted the nuns to like me.

There were two classes in the first grade, each with its own Catholic nun running the show. Nuns were feared and revered. One class had around forty-eight kids, and the other had about fifty, with only one nun for each class. The desks were wooden and uncomfortable. The nun for my class was Sister Josephine Carol or something like that. I thought it was cool that they got to pick their names, and they could have more than one. We never knew if they even had last names.

The days were long and the classes were big, but most kids didn't get out of line. Parents revered the nuns—if a kid did something wrong, or at least wrong in the nun's eyes, the parents typically sided with the nun and the kid got into more trouble at home. There was no second set of eyes or appeal process. And it was mostly the boys that got into trouble.

Nuns could yell, hit kids, and put them in the broom closet with the lights off to scare them, and they got away with it. These were criminal acts, but we were too young to know at the time. There were probably some nice and kind nuns. But in life, most people like me remember most the bad actors.

Since we were only six-years-old in the first grade, we didn't get into much trouble. As we got older, it was another story. The nuns always seemed to be gunning to find someone, usually one of the boys, who did something to get into trouble, even if you didn't know what the kid had done wrong.

There was one punishment where one of the boys would have to stand in the front of the room in view of all the other kids with his arms extended, and the nun would put a heavy book in each hand. The boy wasn't allowed to lower his arms for a long time or the punishment would be worse. Kids cried and were humiliated, and the nuns seemed satisfied with that outcome. Pain and humiliation, a nice daily double, they must have thought. Although I was young, none of that seemed right to me, so I kept very quiet. I didn't want to get noticed by the nuns anymore.

With all of the current gun violence and schools being attacked by student gunmen, there are some people who believe that teachers should be armed with guns in order to protect the students. I don't agree with that at all and am pretty sure that if the nuns who taught my first- or second-grade classes were packing weapons, some of the boys would not have made it past that grade. And most of the Catholic families had a lot of kids, so what was one less?

Grammar school was kind of what incarceration must be like—ugly uniforms, set schedule, nobody could get out of line, and random punishment for practically nothing, or maybe even nothing at all.

The first grade defined what my education would be like until I went to college and defined–and limited–some of my career choices. You see, I am the kid who got written off and thrown away in the first grade and was never expected to ever become anybody.

In the first-grade classroom, everything was written by the nun on the chalkboard in the front of the room. I was seated toward the back. I don't know if the nun intentionally put the boys in the front, but they all seemed to be there. Maybe she thought that the boys' education was more important and that the girls would be housewives anyway.

Back in the early 1960s, they didn't do eye tests on kids before they started school. What nobody realized until after starting the first grade was that I couldn't see the writing on the chalkboard. Although able to hear fine, I couldn't see the board. I learned to read and spell by listening, but that didn't work for math.

When someone at last realized that I couldn't see the writing on the chalkboard, I went to the eye doctor and got glasses. I was very nearsighted, which means I couldn't see the faraway chalkboard. The shiny blue metal frames with the wings seemed to be the most beautiful to me. They were dorky looking, but I only realized that later when I got new ones that were light brown. Apparently my first glasses were not strong enough for me to see, so I got new ones about a year later.

By the time my eyesight issue was resolved, it was too late for me. Math is a subject where you need to learn the simple stuff like addition and subtraction before you can move on to the more complicated areas like fractions and division. It's like building blocks—you need a foundation or they will keep falling over. Since I didn't have that strong foundation, I was lost, and the class was too big for anyone to help me catch up.

The first-grade classes were broken up into four tracks, and each kid was assigned to a track based on the nun's assessment of their intelligence. The tracks were based on the letters READ. The nuns thought they were so clever and had scrambled the letters, thinking the kids wouldn't figure it out, but we all did. The smartest kids, according to the nuns, were in the E track, the next smartest were in the A track, then came the D track, and lastly the R track.

They put me in the D track because I couldn't do math and was too far behind since I couldn't see the chalkboard to begin with. All the kids called the D track the dummy track, and I won't even say what they called the R track. I wasn't dumb, but they decided that I was. Thankfully, my parents weren't disappointed in me. They were happy to be my parents and to have their daughter, Eileen.

Kids could be mean to other kids and that continued well into grammar school. I had glasses and freckles and worried the kids would call me four eyes and freckle-face Flaherty. I tried a couple of times going to the laundry room at home in the basement and taking bleach to my arms to try to get rid of the freckles. It didn't work. I was lucky, though, that the other kids left me alone and didn't make fun of me. I still hated my freckles, but I came to appreciate them later in life.

The first grade wasn't all bad. On Friday night, when the school week was over and I had made it through, my brother and I got to pick what we each wanted for dinner. It was always the same thing for me—macaroni and cheese, the kind in the blue box. To this day, after a rough week, I wait until Friday night and pull out the blue box and it all seems better. There were also the weekends, and Saturday was my favorite day of the week.

There was no D track on the weekends. We usually got a carry-out pizza for dinner on Saturdays with the cold leftovers and a Pepsi for Sunday breakfast. That is still my favorite breakfast, although I don't let myself eat it much anymore.

At the end of the first grade, there was the summer to look forward to. Kids didn't study in the summer and didn't take classes. You were supposed to play and have fun and not focus on learning. Most of the other girls on the block had sisters that they hung out with, but I did wonder if they didn't want to play with me because I was in the D track at school. They weren't mean to me or anything, but I still wondered. With only one brother and no sisters, I mostly kept to myself. I played with my Barbie and rode my bike on the sidewalk. And we went to Wisconsin Dells for a few days for a perfect summer.

Then September came, and it was all over. Back to the D track.

The routine was the same, but second grade was special because you had to prepare to make your First Holy Communion, which was a big deal. It was the only thing that I liked about school at that point. It was a sacrament in the Catholic Church that happened to take place in the second grade. I don't know if it was a rule or anything. There were months of preparation for the First Holy Communion. We had to learn all the religious stuff and practice, practice, practice.

There were no school uniforms for the event (at least for the girls), but we had to wear some nice white dresses and, of course, a veil to cover our heads. I never knew why, but girls and women had to have their heads covered in church at that time. For Sunday mass, if you forgot a hat, you had to put a Kleenex tissue or something to cover your head. I was happy about the hat rule for this day since my veil was so beautiful and special. The boys weren't as lucky—their blue pants and a white short-sleeved shirt were boring, like their uniforms.

My mom and I spent a lot of time shopping for my dress, shoes, and socks. I think I even had new First Holy Communion underwear. My mom wanted everything to be perfect for me. She picked, with my input, the most beautiful white dress. It had a full skirt and short sleeves and my veil matched it. I had always wondered what had happened to that beautiful veil. I assumed my parents must have thrown it out as I'd gotten older.

My First Holy Communion was a very positive event in school for me, and those were rare. What was even better was that the kids got to sit alphabetically and not in the track that the nun had chosen for them. There was no D track for me on First Holy Communion Day. I think, at that point, it was the best day of my life and one that I would always remember.

In the second grade, I joined the Brownies. It was an after-school thing that was run by some volunteer mothers, and the nuns had nothing to do with it. There were about fifteen kids in my troop, and we had uniforms of brown dresses and orange beanie caps. The girl who lived across the street from me in Burbank, Kathy, joined with me to be a Brownie. We were so proud of our uniforms, not realizing at the time how ridiculous we looked.

When the third grade came around, I became a Girl Scout. We had green dresses for uniforms and no beanie caps. The big deal about the uniform was that there was a sash from your shoulder to your waist. You could earn badges, which demonstrated that you had mastered a new skill, and have your mom sew them on the sash so everyone would know that you had a badge. Typically, the girls worked to get a badge every three months or so. Not me. I was so interested and worked hard to get a badge each month.

To earn a badge, you had to learn a topic and do a project or make a presentation. There was no guarantee that you would get a badge just because you were trying. But I got every single one that I tried for. The troop leaders didn't know that I was in the D track, and that let me prove myself on the merits. I stayed in the Girl Scouts until I had all the badges that were interesting to me.

It was amazing how that D track followed me all through grade school. I didn't study much and wasn't interested in school because what was the point? The nuns decided I was in the D track, and that was where I would have to stay.

In the sixth grade, I tried to get into a higher track. My best friend was in that track, so I was going for it. Working harder than ever, I thought it was going to happen. Then when it came time, I got good grades and showed them to the teacher, but she said I wasn't ready. She was wrong, but I stopped trying since they were never going to let me get to that next higher step.

Why did they do that to me?

At some point, they stopped doing the tracks, so technically I wasn't in the D track anymore, but it was all pretty much the same. At age six, I was trapped and carried that stigma with me for a long time.

CHAPTER THREE

QUEEN OF PEACE

It was 1972 and time for me to go to high school. Once again, there were two high schools in Burbank—the Catholic girl's school, Queen of Peace, and the public school, Reavis.

Unlike in grammar school, some of the Catholics went to the public school because the Catholic school cost money for the tuition, and it wasn't cheap. Some of my friends were going to the public school, and I wanted to go there too.

The main attraction for me was that there were no uniforms. I had worn a stupid, scratchy, ugly wool uniform for eight years and was sick of it. My parents wouldn't hear of me going to Reavis, so I was going to Queen of Peace. My dad had to work hard to pay for the tuition as it was a lot of money for us. Their decision was the right one, but I wished that I could have gone with my friends and not worn a uniform.

I had no real interest in high school as it seemed that the teachers treated me the same as the nuns and teachers did in grammar school. I suspected that my grade-school record got transferred to each next grade and the new teacher for that year heard that I was dumb. I didn't study or work hard at school because, like the last eight years of my life, what was the point? The teachers probably looked at me and thought I wasn't going to go anywhere and would likely work in the local grocery store or someplace after high school, get married, have kids, and then send them to Queen of Peace. Well, that was never going to happen, I thought at the time, but there was no point in ever having that discussion with them.

The teachers in my high school were trying an experiment, which ended after I had graduated. They should never have done it. The school had something called modular classes where you had to take certain classes but you could pick the other ones. Some days, there were several hours when you were free to do whatever you wanted within the school. The teachers pitched it that kids could use the hours to focus on subjects that interested them.

What a load of garbage that was.

I suspected that the real idea was so they could have more free time to do nothing. What kind of high school gives freshmen girls hours to do whatever they wanted? Not caring about school at this point, I took sewing and stupid classes, while the other kids were taking calculus and biology. I don't remember anyone at the high school consulting with my parents, so I got to make those decisions on my own.

Since I assumed that I wasn't good at schoolwork, cheerleading became my passion. I was a cheerleader for one of the local Catholic boys' high schools, and there were homecomings and proms. That was all fun and took my mind off school. With all of that free time in school, I decided to make very good use of it.

One day, I thought I should find a way to leave the building several days a week and go home for lunch and watch a soap opera. Of course, none of this was allowed. I gave it a lot of thought and looked for likely exit routes. I finally found a courtyard with a gate that wasn't locked, and it led to a street on the side of the school. I tried opening it for a few days to get up my nerve, and luckily, each time it opened, no alarm went off. I knew that it would be risky to carry out my plan, but lunch at home and *All My Children* seemed worth it.

I was all set and picked the first day for my escape. I was so nervous, shaking and looking over my shoulder afraid of getting caught. I opened the gate and the alarm didn't go off and went right out and walked fast down the street.

It worked.

SpaghettiOs and *All My Children* in the middle of the day were perfect. My mom was glad to have me home and it was a blast. I told her that the school didn't mind if you go home for lunch, as long as it isn't far, and you were back in time for the afternoon classes.

I think she suspected that wasn't the case, but she was glad to have me home spending time watching TV with her. Each day, the gate wasn't locked and I was able to slide right back in after my lunch. This went on for months and then one day in the winter I went to leave for lunch and the gate had a lock on it.

Hmmm.

Since I wasn't spending much time studying, another escape route was needed. My freedom for those few hours was so wonderful that I had to find another gate or door without a lock. There weren't any logical exits so there was only one choice. It was a bold move and I was nervous about it, but one day I walked to the front door of the school, where the principal's office was and the other administrative staff, and went out the door and no alarm went off. If the principal or any other staff had watched me, they would have seen me walk out and right down the street, but they didn't.

Then one day the principal came out to the hall as I was about to head out the front door to leave for lunch and watch TV.

"Where do you think you're going?" she asked.

I froze. Busted. I had to think fast.

"I wanted to get some fresh air," I said.

"Not through that door, you're not," she said.

I had to go back through the hallways and had no lunch or money, so I was starving that day.

The other doors in the building had guards to monitor, so my nice routine of SpaghettiOs and *All My Children* came to an abrupt end. I thought about trying to climb out a window or something to escape, but that seemed too likely to attract attention. I had enjoyed my free time, but sadly, sometimes good things do come to an end.

I finished my sophomore year in high school and then started junior year and had never been to the school library. What was the point? I knew where it was, but I wasn't spending any of my time there and none of the teachers cared.

In the hallways and lunchroom, I started to hear some of the other girls talking about where they were going to college. My brother was in college, and I had always assumed that was my direction too. I started to think about colleges and thought it should be a school that was somewhere warm and fun. I found the school counseling office and went to discuss my options. The woman in charge explained to me that unless I did something immediately to improve my grade point average, there wouldn't be any college for me.

That one took me by surprise.

After that conversation, I went straight to the library and became a serious student in all of my classes. I worked hard to pull up my grades and was doing better, except for math; damn that first grade and everything that followed because of it. After months of studying hard and improving all of my other grades, I then went to the counseling office to start looking at brochures of colleges.

There was no internet at the time, so unless you knew about a school from someone, you went through college brochures and catalogs. I found a school that looked nice, Loras College, and called the school to ask if they would accept someone with my grades. The head of the admissions office said that it would be a stretch and I would have to keep up my grades to get in, so I kept trying.

I went to my parents and told them that Loras College was where I wanted to go to school next. They didn't think it was a good idea and said that I should go to secretarial school instead. I knew that I would not be a good secretary and would likely end up in jail for intentionally spilling hot coffee on some stupid boss. I pleaded to go to college and begged them for a chance to prove myself. They still weren't sure about it, but I didn't give up.

My mom agreed to drive me to see Loras, which is in Dubuque, Iowa. It looked like a nice school, like in the brochure, and had about two thousand students. There were rolling green hills, and Dubuque looked like a nice small college town. It had what seemed like the right number of students so I wouldn't get lost like in a bigger state school. My mom liked it too.

Although I didn't know it at the time, selecting Loras College would turn out to be the turning point in my education and life.

After many discussions with my parents, they agreed that I could go to Loras if I paid half of the tuition and room and board. Having no money, I was determined to get part-time jobs and somehow figure out a way to pay for my half. It wasn't that my parents were cheap or anything, but I had wasted most of my time in high school, and their tuition money, and they wanted me to work hard in college to prove myself and have skin in the game.

Yeah, I was going to college and Loras it was.

CHAPTER FOUR

LORAS

Everything was so different about college. You had to go to grammar school and high school, but you didn't have to go to college. It was a choice. And for me, it almost didn't happen. I was determined to hit the ground running and do my very best at it. I spent the summer working at the local swimming pool to earn money for school and thinking about how lucky I was to be going to college. I thought a lot about what types of clothes college kids would be wearing. I packed and then did it several times again.

College, here I come.

Loras was the best choice for me. It was in Dubuque, Iowa, which, by the way, is not a warm city. In fact, it is freezing in the winter. It was a simple school with one cafeteria and one library, and there were a few dorms.

In my college, the admissions office picked the dorm roommate for you through some type of lottery system. That made me nervous because, if it didn't work out, it could be a miserable year since the rooms were so small. They sent me the name of my roommate by mail, of course, since there was no e-mail. Her name was Cindy, and they gave me her phone number. We talked a few times, and I liked her and knew that we would get along well. She was funny and we laughed a lot.

It was late August 1976, when my parents and I packed the car with my stuff and drove off to college. It was all so exciting. Cindy had gotten there a little bit before I did, so she helped me move in. I brought tons of clothes, not knowing what was best. Cindy and I kept hauling all of it and dropping piles of clothes, which made us laugh even harder. The puddles of rain didn't help either, but nothing was going to spoil this day. It was time for my parents to leave, and this was it—college was starting the next day.

That night, Cindy and I got to know the other gals on our dorm floor, and I liked all of them. Most of us came from the same type of middle-class background and were happy to be there. Cindy and I walked around to figure out where the classes and cafeteria were.

I was most interested in knowing where the library was since I was planning on spending a lot of time there. The cafeteria served the standard cheap carb diet, which we all ate and loved and gained the typical freshmen ten to fifteen pounds.

On the first day of college, I was nervous, but still so excited. I took the standard load of classes in my first semester. One of the classes was political science, and I thought maybe it could be interesting.

I got to the classroom early and made sure to get a seat in the second row in the front of the room. No more back rows for me because I was there to learn. I picked the second row thinking maybe the first row would be too close to the front if the professor moved around. It was the perfect spot for me, and I thought it was a good start to my new strategy of actually wanting to be in school and learn. When the class started, that was immediately it.

That day my life changed forever.

The professor's name was Dr. Bill C. Cermack, and we called him Doc Mak.

"Hello, class. I'm Doc Mak, and I have one question before we start. Do any of you want to go to law school and become a lawyer?" he said.

I slowly raised my hand—me, from the D track in the first grade. Nobody is going to believe that I could be a lawyer.

Doc Mak looked straight at me.

"Well, you look like you're smart enough, and I am going to help you get to law school," he said.

Did he just say that?

It was unbelievable to me. He didn't know my past and that I was a D track kid. He looked at me and believed in me, even though he didn't even know me. He was the first teacher that I could remember who did this. My gratitude overwhelmed me. To this day, I think about Doc Mak often. He made a huge difference in my life and opened a door for me that no other teacher ever had.

I listened intently to every word that he said in class and took good notes. When the class was over, I walked back to the dorm.

What in the heck happened?

Doc Mak was the first teacher to believe in me. He was giving me an opportunity to be somebody and, in that very moment, I committed that I was not going to let him down. No matter what, that was not going to happen.

I can't let what happened in the first grade pull me down again.

I worked hard at every class and was getting all A's, except in math. Diane lived in the dorm room next door and heard about my difficulty with math.

"I can't learn math," I told her.

She was a whiz at it. "Yes, you can," she said.

"No, I can't," I said honestly.

Diane vowed to help me get through it and pass. I was in the math class at Loras that everyone called "sandbox math." You were required to take a college math class, and mine was the lowest level that you could take. I wasn't discouraged at that and didn't let it label me this time around. I worked and studied, and it wasn't easy. I was getting a C in math and eventually worked hard enough to pull it up to a B. Of all of my grades, I think that was the one I was most proud of.

Me, Eileen, got a B in math.

I was so energized by learning in college and decided after the first semester to attempt the unthinkable—I was going to try to graduate from Loras in three years instead of the standard four years. I thought it could save me a full year of tuition and room and board, and maybe I could use the money for law school if I got into one.

That was it. There was no looking back. I studied all the time, spent a lot of time in the library, did every extra credit assignment, and kept going. There were plenty of semesters when I had three finals in one day and would stay up nights to do the best I could.

I went out with school friends to the bars in Dubuque occasionally, but not that much. I was lucky to discover during the first few weeks that I hated beer, and Dubuque, Iowa, was big on beer. There was no decent wine around there, or at least none that I found, which made it easy for me to stay in on weekends and study.

My big Saturday night treat while I was in, studying, was a pack of Hostess Ho Hos, with vanilla or whatever it was in the layers, and a Mountain Dew from the vending machine in the dorm basement. I needed a buzz from the caffeine and sugar to stay up all night studying. I didn't mind at all except the basement was empty, dark and kind of creepy down there. I always got the heck out of there as fast as I could.

Another time that I remember well in college was when I was back in Chicago for Christmas break and there was a huge snowstorm. I was supposed to take the bus back to school, and my dad was going to drive me to the bus station in Chicago. The storm was bad, but I had to get back to school and the bus was the only way to get there.

As we were about to leave the house, my dad said, "I'm driving you back to school."

"No way, it's a four-hour drive on a good day, and you'll have to drive all the way back by yourself," I said.

"I'm doing it. I want to make sure that you get there safely."

It is one of the strongest memories I have—that he was willing to do that for me. The drive from Chicago back to Loras was dangerous, and we took it slow. One of the girls in my dorm was sadly killed that day on the way back to school when a semi-truck slipped on the ice and rammed into the back of the car where she was sitting.

During the drive, it kept snowing hard and the roads were slippery. My dad wanted to get me a nice dinner, but all I wanted was an A&W hamburger and a root beer float, so that is where we went. He had to drive all the way back by himself, but he never complained about doing it.

I was so glad to be in the car with my dad on that long ride. You see, he was almost killed when I was in the fifth grade. His job with the electric company required him to climb the utility poles that had electric wires, which is how people got electricity to their houses. He often had to work days in a row with no sleep when there was a storm that knocked out the power in the neighborhoods of Chicago.

One late night, my brother and I were still up and my mom got a call. She started to cry.

Something was wrong.

"What is going on?" we both asked.

"I have to go to the hospital. Your dad has been electrocuted on the job, and I don't know if he'll be okay," she said.

My brother and I begged to go with her, but she said we were too young to get into the hospital. I think it was more that she didn't know if he was going to make it. It was the four of us in our family. My brother and I stayed home waiting for her for hours with me crying and us worrying about him and what would happen to our family.

Please don't die, Dad. Please.

After hours of my brother and I worrying and waiting, my mom came home exhausted. She said that his condition was serious; his heart had stopped and he had to be revived.

But she said the words we needed to hear. "The doctors think he will be okay."

He was in the hospital for many days and I worried all the time. When he finally came home, I could see that he was weak but was going to be okay. I was so relieved to have him home and with us. On that long ride back to Loras during the snowstorm, I was reminded of how grateful I was to have both of my parents. Life would not have been the same if he had died that day.

College was all going well for me except that I had a part-time job to help pay for my half of the tuition and room and board, and it was taking too much time away from my schoolwork. I was a lifeguard in the evenings at the community swimming pool near campus. It wasn't hard work, but I couldn't study while I was at work since I didn't want anyone to drown on my watch. It didn't feel safe walking back to my dorm at night. It wasn't a dangerous city, Dubuque, but I had to cross a huge snowy field at night during the winter by myself, or I always hoped that I was by myself. I never told my parents about having to walk by myself at night through that empty field because I knew they would worry too much.

One day early into the second semester of my first year, I called my mom and said that maybe I would have to come home from Loras and go to school at a local junior college and live at home to save money.

"Mom, I can't take all these classes and work at the same time," I said.

She paused. "Do you want to stay there?"

"Yes," I immediately said.

Without hesitation, she said, "Then we'll pay for it."

I wasn't expecting my parents to pay, and I wasn't asking for that, but when she offered, I accepted. She said that I had proven myself during the first semester and that is all she and my dad wanted to see. She always had my back. I will always miss her forever.

I kept studying with the same determination every day. Then it came time in my third year of college to take the test to try to get into law school. I knew that, with my difficulty in math, getting into law school would be a challenge. I always appreciated how my mom worked so hard to keep everything perfect at home and my dad worked so hard to provide for our family. He even worked overtime any chance he could to pay the bills. I think I inherited my strong work ethic from both of them. With the same commitment to make it work, I studied and took the test and passed. Me, Eileen from the D track, was going to law school.

And I did it. I graduated from Loras College in three years with high honors. When my parents came to the graduation, once again I had on a nice dress and wore a cap and gown during the ceremony. I even got a dozen pink roses from my parents. That day was sunny and cool and perfect for a graduation. My friends Cindy, Diane, and Michelle were there to see me graduate, and we had so much fun that day.

When they called my name to go up to the podium and get my college diploma, I was so proud of myself. I had worked so hard from the first day of college, stayed up so many nights to study and had finally achieved something in school. My parents were beaming with pride. It wasn't the First Holy Communion Day or anything, but for a college graduation, it was perfect by me.

I was sad that day to leave my friends because they were staying for the fourth year of college. It finally occurred to me, on that last day, that if I had stayed for the fourth year, it could have been some fun. After graduation, Cindy, Diane and Michelle, kept me company while I was packing to leave. I played the song "Best of Friends" by Boz Scaggs from my vinyl album, and was kind of sad. I had to let those thoughts pass quickly as I was going to law school and had a new focus and drive. They were my close friends and still are. I wasn't going to lose them for good, so it would be okay.

CHAPTER FIVE

LAW SCHOOL

I was going to law school, but once again, didn't know how I was going to pay for it. I decided right after college to go to paralegal school, which would take about six months. I would get a job as a paralegal and work for a law firm and go to law school at night. I realized right after my college graduation that plan was going to take way too long and it wasn't going to save me any money in the long run.

I never asked my parents to pay for law school, but they offered to help me out, and I so appreciated it. They were proud of me for trying to become the first lawyer in our family. They were beaming and telling everyone in Burbank that I was going to law school. I was always so proud of their hard work ethic and determined again to not let them down.

In the months before law school started in January, I worked a series of part-time jobs—an administrative assistant, law clerk, vote checker at the local elections, and just about anything to earn money. My father had been a part-time alderman in our community for thirty-three years until the day he passed away. It was such a source of pride for him, and I was proud of him too. So hard work and multiple jobs to earn money was nothing new to my family.

On the first day of law school, I did the very same thing as the first day in college. I sat toward the front of the class and told myself that I had to be a success and a great lawyer, whatever kind that might be. Some students skipped classes and got others' notes. I calculated, based on how much the course cost, what skipping a class would cost me, and I wasn't going to throw away a nickel. I loved learning all of the courses, even criminal law and property law. And I got top grades throughout those three years of law school.

I worked at the local swimming pool during the summers to pay for school. It was the best job ever, not having to wear shoes all summer and keeping kids in line. Part-time legal jobs were important for students to have, so I also had a series of them all through law school during the school year. One job I had was as a clerk for a law firm, working about fifteen to twenty hours a week. It was tedious work, and the firm billed their clients a fortune and paid me next to nothing. That was the game. You had to play your part and work hard, as law clerking was like an internship. It could eventually help you land a job, or at least serve to get good references.

I studied every weekend, and each week was long with school and work. Every Friday night, that blue box of macaroni and cheese was a savior. I didn't mind the work and school, being grateful to have the opportunity, and I was giving it everything. Besides, having fun on the weekends wasn't going to do anything for my future anyway.

Law school was a smooth sail for me, even though I was working hard. Having taught myself how to study in college that first week, I kept applying the same principles. And there was no math, and nobody even knew that I couldn't do it. This was definitely something that I could be good at, and I was determined to make it happen.

I made the dean's list most semesters, and even won a few awards as the top student in some of my classes. Because of my top grades, I even got a small scholarship one semester. Imagine me getting an academic scholarship. Nobody who ever knew me at St. Albert the Great in the D track would ever believe that someone like me would be able to do this. That didn't matter. I had ripped out that rearview mirror, or at least thought that I had.

When it came time for graduation day, my parents were beaming. They had both come from modest means in Chicago, and my grandparents had immigrated to the United States from Ireland with almost nothing.

So with their humble backgrounds, my parents were so proud of me that day and for my accomplishments. Their daughter was the first lawyer in our family, and they were telling everyone they knew. I was so thrilled about that, given where I had started in the first grade, and that they were so excited for me. And the day wasn't only about me. I was so proud of them. They had sacrificed a lot to make sure that my brother and I had good lives and opportunities.

After graduation from law school, I had to pass the bar, which is a big exam and required if you want to get a job as a lawyer. I had more academic confidence now and thought that maybe I might be able to do it. And there wasn't any math on it, so I had a decent chance. Since I lived in Illinois, I took the bar in downtown Chicago. After the exam, I was nervous because I had had insomnia for the two nights before it and was exhausted because the exam lasted all day for two straight days.

I was afraid that I had a good chance of failing. When someone fails the bar, they can take it again, but everyone knows that they failed.

It was so tense waiting for the results that I couldn't sleep on and off for many nights. It was a few months later, which seemed like an eternity, when the envelope came from the Illinois bar. I was frozen and couldn't open it and didn't tell anyone the day that it came.

What if I failed?

It would be devastating and maybe those feelings of not being good enough would come back. Maybe I wasn't as good as the other students.

I got into my car, an old Mustang, which my brother called "the rustang," and drove around with the letter. I was shaking. With nowhere in particular to go, I went to St. Albert the Great church, not the school, as the church had been a happy place for me with the First Holy Communion Day and everything.

The church was empty, and I sat there by myself for at least an hour or maybe longer. I was not a holy roller or anything and wasn't expecting divine intervention to let me pass the bar. I needed a quiet place with nobody around to process it if I failed. Finally getting up the nerve, I opened the envelope. I kept shaking and couldn't stop. I read it and read it again. I did this so many times trying hard to make sure of what I was seeing through my tears.

I passed the Illinois bar on my first try.

I got back into my car and raced home with the good news. My mom was there.

"I did it, I passed the bar," I said.

She cried tears of joy with me. When my dad got home from work, I could tell that he felt the same, and I could see tears welling up in his eyes.

"I'm so proud of you," he said.

"I am too. We should celebrate," she said.

"Thanks, how about some macaroni and cheese?" I said.

"Don't you want something special?" she asked.

After thinking for a minute, I said, "The blue box has gotten me through this far, so that is all I want, thanks."

For the three years of law school, I had very little money. Dad always filled my car with gas each week so I wouldn't have to pay for it, and mom was always slipping me some cash for lunch and clothes. They were so much a part of my success. The daughter of Therese and Bill Flaherty was a lawyer who passed the bar—and the first one in our family to do it.

With the bar behind me, I now had to get a job as a lawyer, and try to have a big start at my new legal career.

CHAPTER SIX

THE BOZOS

It wasn't that easy to find a legal job since there was no internet or jobsites, which is how the most people get jobs these days. If kids now only knew how hard it was then, they would appreciate how easy they have it now.

While looking for a job, I kept clerking for the small law firm where I worked in law school. I had always worked and wanted to keep doing the same during my search for a job. I lived at home and took the train, which was about thirty minutes into downtown Chicago, and walked another twenty minutes to my law clerking job and did my searches in the evenings and on weekends.

Since I had so little money during law school and after, I had to drive to the train station thirty minutes away and park in the lot that was free. The problem was that it was on the more dangerous side of the railroad tracks. I thought some people probably carried guns for protection, but I didn't have one.

I was always afraid when I got off the train and had to get to my car after 8:00 at night. I didn't have a choice, though. I didn't tell my parents since I didn't want them to worry. And even though they would have paid for me to park in the safe lot a few blocks away, I didn't want to ask.

To help my job search, I would go to the law library when I was downtown and get the law firm reference book that had all of the major law firms in the country. I would pick places where I might want to live and write letters to the law firms there. I didn't have any contacts at law firms or legal departments in corporations because I was the first lawyer in my family.

Landing my first job was a time-consuming and manual process. I would type a letter to each one of the firms and attach my resume, mail it, and hope that it got there. And then I would wait to see if a response came. Sometimes I got one, but mostly I didn't get any responses. When I did get one, the answer was always the same. They were not hiring but would keep my resume on file in case the situation changed.

I sent out dozens and dozens of letters. At the time, there were too many kids coming out with law degrees and not enough jobs for them. It was kind of discouraging, but I had to keep looking to land that first job.

I would mention to anyone and everyone, including strangers, that I was a new law school grad and looking for a job as a lawyer. In the elevators in the building where I clerked, I tried to strike up conversations with anyone to let them know that I was looking for a position. I wasn't embarrassed—I had no other choice. It was hard trying to build a network from scratch, but I had to keep working at it.

After a few months of this, one day, my persistence paid off. I struck up a conversation with a guy in the elevator, and he said that his law firm was looking for a lawyer and that he would consider a new graduate who had some law clerking experience. I told him that I was very interested. I called that day and scheduled an interview. I had never heard of this law firm before and that should have been my first clue that something may be off. But jobs were tight and I couldn't be choosy. They were in the same building where I worked, and I went for the interview.

It was a small firm, Downs and Martenn, that had two partners, Nate Downs and Henry Martenn, and one associate. The partners had very different personalities. The associate was a nice guy and I liked him, but I wasn't sure about the partners. I hadn't heard of them before and they were in the same building where I was clerking. It seemed that they didn't like each other, and their areas of law practice were very different. And I wasn't sure, as a new lawyer, if they would give me the chance to learn and become a good lawyer.

The firm "specialized" in house closings and personal injury lawsuits. They offered me the job and I took it. It paid $18,500 a year, which was a lot of money to me. It was a far cry from my first babysitting job when I was in the sixth grade where I made a dollar an hour babysitting for four energetic kids, or when I was fifteen and made $1.65 an hour at Dunkin' Donuts.

With my huge new salary, I could get a studio apartment downtown, some legal-type clothes, and maybe even save a little. I was very excited to have my first real job as a lawyer in downtown Chicago and eager to start as soon as possible. Henry Martenn said that the associates were expected to work six days a week. I had no problem with that since I wasn't lazy and wanted to learn as much as possible.

I started my new job and it was okay. Not great but okay, and I was still glad to have it. I found a studio apartment about three miles from work and moved out of my parents' house, now making the big bucks. I didn't mind living at home, but with a big job, I wanted my own apartment closer to work and I was always scared walking from the train to my car in the dangerous neighborhood. My apartment was so tiny, I didn't have much furniture, and I slept on a pullout couch, but it was my space, roaches and all.

A friend from college, Carol, got a studio apartment in the same rundown building too. We also got to know another gal in the building, Camille, and the three of us became great friends. Since we were all starting out and none of us had any money saved, we would go to ladies' night at the local bars. We got to have a glass of wine for free. But even better, we ate the cheap hors d'oeuvres and called it dinner. We always tipped the waitresses well, as they were working gals like us. We had a blast.

At the time, in the early eighties, women lawyers were expected to wear a suit like the men, but with a skirt instead of pants. Pants weren't professional enough. I worked up to having a whole week's worth of different shades of navy-blue suits and white button-down collared shirts. And you had to wear a tie, not like the men, but one that you tied at the neck into a bow. Stockings were a must, and they could have no color or white, and my dress shoes matched my suits.

Looking like all of the other women lawyers, I thought I looked nice. It felt like my old school uniforms, but this time I didn't mind. Nobody would be caught dead in that kind of business attire anymore, but that was a time when women were expected to wear that attire to be taken seriously as a professional.

I had never done the legal documents for a house closing before, and Henry assigned several closings to me right away. I read everything, but Henry started to say that I wasn't moving them along quickly enough. Nobody taught me the actual steps to do a house closing. So I was kind of lost but kept trying harder. I was starting to get more and more nervous that he didn't like me.

I worked on some personal injury cases too. They were small cases where someone claimed to have slipped or fallen and the client wanted money for it. I couldn't tell if any of the clients were actually injured, but this law firm was happy to sue the place where the client fell and try to get money.

There was one deposition where I got to sit in on the preparation of the client. In a personal injury case, the insurance company that represents the client on the other side that is getting sued gets to take a formal statement, called a deposition, of the person injured. It was surprising to me that Nate, who was handling the case, seemed to keep reminding the client what his injuries were. The client didn't seem to be stupid, but he couldn't get it right as maybe he didn't have any injuries or at least any that he could remember.

Was this even legal, for a lawyer to tell a client what his injuries were?

If it wasn't illegal, it was in my opinion unethical. That was the kind of sleazy tactics that I saw in that deposition preparation. I didn't get to attend any others.

I went to court for a few cases to argue some motions in front of judges. Motions are early procedural steps in a civil case, but they can have a significant impact on the overall outcome. Here, again, I read everything to teach myself how to present a motion in court. Nobody taught me how to do this, so it was all on me. I worked at it using my study skills from college and law school. Practicing many times in front of the bathroom mirror at my apartment helped me to see how I was presenting and kept improving.

There was one case where I had to go to court and argue an important motion in front of a judge. I was still a new lawyer trying to improve my skills with every chance. The lawyer representing the client on the other side of the case would have to argue in front of the same judge, a position that was opposite to the one I was arguing. He looked young too, but I got the sense that he had more experience than I had.

I looked around the courtroom and noticed how formal it was. In the front of the room, the judge was seated on a raised platform with a desk in front of him. There was an American flag off to the side but still very noticeable. There was also a large symbol with the city seal or something like that. I didn't have time to take it all in as this was it, my first real argument to present a motion in a courtroom.

As the court clerk started to call the case, I approached the judge's bench and the other lawyer did the same. I was so nervous to be doing an important motion in the case and worried that I wouldn't do well or somehow trip up in my presentation.

Be your best and don't let anyone know how nervous you are, I told myself.

As I was closer to the bench, I started to notice that some of the older lawyers in the courtroom were taking seats in the front rows. They wanted to see the young lawyers duke it out. The law was old stuff to them, but we were both young and we seemed to be the show to watch that day.

Surprisingly, after looking around a bit, it gave me more confidence. In looking at the older guys in the front rows, I thought if they were nice enough to spend their time watching us, I had to be on my game. Like they say in sports, play like you've been there before.

The clerk of the court called the case. The courtroom became quiet and then it was time. I presented my motion and argument first. There was nobody from Downs and Martenn who bothered to come and see me and whether I had any courtroom skills. I was there by myself and thought it had gone pretty well. The other lawyer went next. He was good and, of course, his side of the case was better than mine. I got to do a rebuttal and made it as compelling as possible.

Oh well, he won and I lost.

He deserved to win since his case was better. Before leaving the courtroom, a few of the older lawyers stopped and told me what a great job I had done. I thanked them for their kind words and said that this was my first big motion ever. They were impressed and I was proud of that and still am. If my parents had been there, they would have been telling everyone in the courtroom that I was their daughter.

I wasn't learning much at this law firm unless I taught it to myself, and I came to realize that neither of the partners cared about me or my career. The associate was nice and smart, but they worked him like a dog and he didn't have time to help me. I started to understand that they wanted cheap labor from a lawyer to make more money for themselves and that this personal injury stuff wasn't for me. I concluded these guys were bozos. This job was not going to advance my career, but it was a job, and jobs were scarce. So I kept at it six days a week.

This went on for almost six months. Then one day, Henry, whom I liked the least, called me into his office and said, "We're letting you go."

Fired?

"You aren't picking up the house closings fast enough, and we need someone with more experience," he said.

I couldn't believe this was actually happening to me.

It took everything in me to maintain my composure and not show any emotion. I couldn't let him have that satisfaction of seeing me upset. That was a lesson I had to apply several more times in my career. I learned, at that moment in my life, there was no point in engaging in a conversation when a decision had already been made. They gave me no severance, but Henry said that I could stay for a few weeks while I looked for a job. I was upset but didn't let those bozos know.

Walking home from the office that night, I was devastated. When far enough away where they couldn't see me, I started to cry. This was my first job as a lawyer, and I got fired. What would I tell my parents, and what would they think? I knew that they would worry about me.

They had told everyone in Burbank that I was a lawyer at a downtown Chicago law firm. They wouldn't have been disappointed in me and never were, but I was too embarrassed and didn't know what to do. Was I going to have to move back home or somehow be able to pay for my studio apartment? It was awful going into the office each day, but I needed the money.

I wished that I could have afforded to leave and tell them to fuck off.

After two weeks, Nate came to my office and asked, "How is the job search going?"

"I'm working as hard as I can to find a job," I said.

After thinking about it, I decided, well, fuck them. Working there wasn't going to do anything for my career as a lawyer and that, in the long run, I had more to offer than house closings and slip-and-fall cases with, in my opinion, questionable injuries. I decided that I had worked too hard to settle for this kind of a job in my career and had to pick myself up again. I had to tell myself that it would be okay even if it didn't feel like it at that point.

I was back to looking for a job and wondering how to explain that my first job was only for six months. Surely, I thought anyone who would get my resume would know that I was fired and they wouldn't want to hire me. That was a tough time, but I had to rise above it and keep going. Nate and Henry broke up the law firm not long after I got fired, and each went their separate ways. That was too bad as they deserved each other.

Self-doubt started to come again, and I thought maybe I wasn't good enough. Those are strong feelings and even when you think you have overcome them, they can creep back in before you know it. So even though I had found my confidence, this event in my life was taking me back. Sure, they were bozos, but I was the kid from the D track and maybe I wasn't good enough to be a lawyer. I made it, or maybe I got lucky enough to fake it, but I had to figure out what to do next.

CHAPTER SEVEN
A TRIP TO WALL STREET

While I was desperately searching for a job to get away from the bozos, a friend of mine mentioned that Morgan Lipton was looking for some stockbrokers and maybe I should try that. I was so proud to be a lawyer and had worked hard to get there and pass the bar and everything. My parents were so proud of their daughter in the downtown Chicago law firm. And all the part-time jobs clerking and killing myself to get great grades and succeed, should I give all of that up? But I thought about it and sent my resume to Morgan Lipton anyway.

I got a call to go for an interview there and went to meet with the head of the Morgan Lipton office on Wacker Drive in Chicago, Tim Walton. It was an impressive office space with a ticker-tape machine that everyone in the main room could see. There seemed to be a lot of energy going on in that place.

In the main room, there were many brokers who had desks, and they all seemed to be busy on the phones. There were offices along the walls for what must have been the more experienced brokers. After leaving their offices and still not being sure whether this was what I wanted to do for a career, it was going to take a lot of thought.

A few days later, Tim called and offered me the job. It paid $25,000 a year. That was a big leap from what the law firm paid, and I never imagined making that kind of money. After my last job, I thought I would have to take a pay cut to get a new one.

If I took the job, they had told me that the new hires would get to go to New York City for a month to get some training. Other than my grandparents, who immigrated to the United States, with my grandmother getting processed through Ellis Island right off of the tip of New York City, nobody in my family had ever been there, so I thought this could be cool to try. And maybe this law thing wasn't for me anyway.

I had applied to a labor law firm right out of school, and I wanted that job. They gave it to a guy, and the head partner told me that he would have to support a family someday, so they picked him. At least he was honest and I appreciated that he had the integrity to call me and explain why I didn't get it.

And now my first job as a lawyer was over, having been fired within six months by two, in my opinion, bozos. My confidence was shaken. So I decided to leave the law and try to be a stockbroker and thought that if I didn't like it, I could go back to law. Then my resume would make sense as it would look like I left the law to be a stockbroker and then decided to go back. I thought that this strategy had a chance.

When I told my parents about being a stockbroker, I could tell that they were not thrilled about me giving up my law career. I explained to them how much money they were going to pay me and didn't tell them that I was fired from my first job as a lawyer. They still supported my decision, and I always appreciated that.

Packing for the big trip to New York was exciting after having bought some fancy new clothes to be a stockbroker. I flew to New York for my one month of training, and that was amazing. Morgan Lipton was the most prestigious brokerage firm in the country. Nobody came near them, and I thought this name couldn't hurt my resume. It is also amazing now how the number one brokerage firm in the country isn't heard of anymore.

New York was unbelievably cool. Morgan Lipton put all of the trainees in a dump of a hotel near Grand Central Station, and we had to share a room with other brokers in training. The room was dark and dingy. My roommate, Valerie, I thought, was pretty phony. She seemed to be jealous of me since she had to study so hard while it came easier for me, particularly the presentations. I would go out for dinner with some of the other brokers in training and she would stay behind to study.

I later learned that someone was spreading rumors about me partying too much. I didn't at all. I went to dinner with a few of the other brokers, always in a group, and didn't stay out late. I thought Valerie might be the one spreading the rumors but there wasn't anything I could do about it, so I ignored the bitch. That seemed to make her angrier, and I liked that.

We took the subway trains every day during the week from Grand Central Station down to Wall Street since their offices were a block away from the World Trade Center. We spent some time on the trading floor of the New York Stock Exchange learning about how stocks are traded and what market makers do on the floor of the Exchange. It was so interesting, and I was glad to be there. New York City wasn't very clean at the time and it was dense, but it was busy and exciting.

On the weekends, we were free to go and see New York. I made the most of every minute seeing Central Park, Grand Central Station, Fifth Avenue, Rockefeller Center, the Statue of Liberty, and the World Trade Center. After a month, our training was over and it was time to go back to Chicago to apply my new stockbroker skills. I left New York glad that I'd gotten the opportunity and thought I should go back there at some point since it had such a buzz.

Back in Chicago at the Morgan Lipton offices on Wacker Drive, I was assigned to a desk and given some reading materials and a phone book with all of the names and phone numbers of the people in Chicago and the surrounding suburbs. But the message was clear. It was time to generate stockbroker business. The party was over rather fast. At that time, you used a phone book or some personal contacts and tried to catch clients and reel them in to open an account and buy stocks from you.

Not yet having a knack for picking stocks, I looked at municipal bonds. I focused on high-quality municipal bonds where there was very little risk to the client and they would get interest income. I didn't want to risk my reputation by selling risky stocks where a client could lose money, although I didn't have much of a reputation yet. None of the other stockbrokers used this approach. Many of the others were focused on how much in commissions they could generate for themselves each day.

That wasn't very ethical to me, to not put the client's interests first, and I wasn't going to do that. My mom and dad would not be happy if I had ever acted unethically, so I didn't. That was not how my parents raised me. They were always honest and I was too.

All of the stockbrokers' commission numbers were reported to Tim every day. I was only a few months into this new stockbroker job, and I had weekly meetings with Tim and everyone else did too. He was nice enough but not too friendly. He wanted to know how the prospecting for clients was going and what I thought my potential in commissions was going to be. I made up answers to buy some time to figure this thing out and whether I was going to be any good at it. I was bringing in some clients, but I actually hated it.

After the first few weeks back from New York, the thrill was gone, and as time went by, I realized this was a crappy job of cold calling strangers, trying to get them to open stock accounts. While I had some success, it was not a lot, and I loathed every minute of it. But I didn't want to get fired—I couldn't let that happen to me again.

After a few more weeks, I hated that job so much. I wanted to be a practicing lawyer again and always had. To me, being a stockbroker was just sales and some people were good at it, but I was a lawyer in the wrong job.

So, I thought of the saying on my family crest, which is a symbol from Ireland. "Fortune Favors the Bold." I've always loved that. So, I would have to be bold now and figure this thing out.

What am I going to do?

Being the first lawyer in my family was something that I was proud of, and my parents were too. I realized that the only reason I had taken the job was that those two bozos from that law firm had shaken my confidence. Why should I let them keep me from doing what I wanted most to do? Maybe I wasn't cut out for a legal career doing house closings and slip-and-fall cases where I wasn't sure if there were any real injuries.

Professor Doc Mak had confidence in me the first day in his class in college when I decided to do of all the work that it took to become a lawyer. I finally got my confidence back and decided that I was capable of more and should go back and find a good legal job this time.

I would have to move fast because time was running out in my current job. With my focus calling, I wasn't bringing in much stockbroker business. I had to find my way back to the law.

CHAPTER EIGHT
NATIONAL DERIVATIVES
ASSOCIATION

I didn't know how to go about finding another legal job, and sending out more letters and resumes seemed like such a waste of time with likely no results. Then one day, while still working as a stockbroker, I called a law professor from my former law school. Never having taken his class, I took a chance that maybe he would take my call.

To my surprise, he answered his own phone and talked to me even though he didn't know me. His name was Ron, and I told him what I was doing in the financial markets and that I wanted to get back into law.

That call was that second door that opened for me in my life, and it gave me the opportunity for a good and long career, which I didn't have at the time.

He was such a great guy. He said that he was on the Board of Directors of the National Derivatives Association, the self-regulator in the derivatives industry. I wasn't even sure what that was.

"Call over there and use my name. Tell them you're interested in a position as a staff lawyer," Ron said.

"Thank you so much, Ron, for taking the time to talk to me, and I'm going to call them right now," I said.

I called the NDA and explained to one of the senior lawyers there my experience in the financial markets and that I was a lawyer. I didn't oversell myself and have never done that in my career, but they seemed impressed that I knew something about the markets. As luck would have it, they were looking for a junior attorney, and we set up an interview.

Their offices were beautiful and right in downtown Chicago, on Jackson Street, and the people that I interviewed with were nice. I was hoping to get the job and was thrilled when they offered it to me. And I was more shocked when they gave me a salary of $30,000 a year.

It was 1984, and this was a huge amount of money for me. Remember, my first job was as a babysitter at a dollar an hour, so making this much now was unbelievable. I was getting back to my true calling as a lawyer and going to be paid a fortune to do it. I didn't think anything could ever be better.

I was going to be a derivatives lawyer and not doing some stupid house closings or "slip-and-fall" cases. I had never heard of lawyers specializing in derivatives and didn't know much about it at the time. Derivatives are traded on some of the largest exchanges in the world, and they can be used for speculation and hedging farm products and other things. I just so happened to fall into it, and it would become my career-long specialty many years later.

To this day, Ron and I are great friends. I was so lucky that he took my call that day and helped me get my first job as a derivatives lawyer. I am so grateful to Ron for helping me get the direction and that one chance to get started in my real profession. When that door opened, I ran through it and never looked back at the bozos or the stockbroker business.

I am forever grateful to Ron for it. To this day, he truly is one of the best people I will ever know.

The job at the NDA was fantastic, and I liked the people there. I was working five days a week, not six, but put in plenty of extra time in order to learn and contribute as much as I possibly could. I was an okay writer, but I became a much better writer with the supervision of the more senior attorneys.

One day, not long after I finished my first few assignments, one of the senior lawyers there told me that I had to work harder to become a better writer. My feelings were hurt, but he was right. I worked at it during work hours and in the evenings and on weekends. They actually taught me stuff there, unlike the bozos. I got to write regulatory rules and memos and participate in big cases where a regulated entity did something wrong. And then there were the arbitrations. Oh, I loved the arbitrations.

The arbitration program was there for when a customer of an NDA-regulated firm sues them because they lost money. Nobody ever sued a firm if they made money. was a relatively new organization formed in 1981, they wanted an attorney to be there at each arbitration hearing to make sure that everything was fair.

The best part was that the customers were located all over the country and the arbitrations were typically held in the cities where the customers lived. There were a lot of shady firms in California at the time, so many of the arbitrations were held in California. Since the other young lawyers had kids, we would trade cases. I would give them my Michigan or Kansas City and trade for anywhere farther like San Francisco, Seattle, and Texas.

I was making $30,000 a year as a lawyer and getting free trips to arbitrations and free dinners in restaurants. I was so happy to have that job, I thought it didn't get better than this. I think I was in California more than ten times in two years and had two trips to Seattle and a bunch of other cool places I'd never been before.

As a kid, my parents took us to the Wisconsin Dells every year during the summers, except for once when we got to go to Washington, DC, where we saw the United States Supreme Court building. I was sure I wanted to go back there at some point in my life. Who knew that one day I would make it back to Washington, DC, to be sworn into the United States Supreme Court Bar?

One year, we even went to the Expo 67, which was a world's fair held that year in Montreal, Canada. And now with this job at the NDA, I was seeing so many different cities and someone was paying me to do it. What a blast! Who would ever want to leave a job like this?

CHAPTER NINE
THE REAL LAW FIRM

I liked my job at the NDA and the people who worked there and especially the trips to the arbitrations. It was such a nice place, and some of my best friends still work there. And they were paying me $30,000 a year, which was more money than I thought I could ever make. It was plenty to pay for my studio apartment, more navy-blue suits, and to be able to save a little. I think, at this point, there were ten navy-blue suits in my closet. Lawyers were told to wear navy suits since it was thought to be a sincere color for a lawyer. The job was great.

For some reason, after two years, I thought that I should look around to see what other jobs there might be out there for me. I knew that it would be taking a risk if I left, but to advance my career, I was going to have to take some risks. And since fortune favors the bold, I thought this was what I should be doing. And, oh boy, through the years, I sure took some risky moves and even risks within moves.

I sent my resume to a premier Chicago law firm, Franklin and Abrams, that specialized in derivatives. That is because I was now a derivatives lawyer and actually knew something about it. Most of the famous lawyers in derivatives had worked at that law firm at some point in their careers. I didn't think there was any chance of me getting that job, but I had nothing to lose by sending in my resume. I had my confidence back, so if they rejected me, it would be fine.

To my surprise, I got a call to go there for an interview. Wow, that was a good first step. If they were going to reject me, they wouldn't bring me in to meet with the other lawyers to do it. I met with two partners, Liz and Reggie,

..g my interviews. I liked both of them, and they seemed to like me. To this day, one of them, Liz, is one of my closest friends.

Then I met with the head partner, John Franklin. I was very nervous since he was so well known and respected for his legal skills. And he looked like a lawyer with his silver hair and professional appearance. The conversation started out with some small talk, and it was just the two of us in his big office. I remember how impressive it was.

Then John asked me some questions about my current job and why I wanted to leave it. I explained that career progression was the reason since my current job at the NDA was fine. He agreed that career progression was important but then asked questions that seemed odd to me.

"What church do you go to on Sunday?"

He was Irish and must have been a practicing Catholic and wanted to know if I was one too.

I had to think fast as I didn't go to church on Sundays at that point in my life.

"Holy Name Cathedral on State Street," I said.

"What mass do you go to on Sundays," he asked?

Oh boy, I was in trouble. I remembered after walking past that church so many times on my way home from work that they had a sign with the times of the Sunday masses. Without hesitation, I said, "The 9:30 mass."

I started thinking, "Oh shit, what if he asks me the names of the priests?" Luckily, he didn't or my cover would have been blown.

I didn't feel good about not telling the truth to John, but I got over it since he probably shouldn't have asked me those questions anyway. I wasn't offended or anything, but I am pretty sure nobody asks those types of questions on interviews anymore.

They hired me and I even got a small increase in salary. I was going to be working for Franklin and Abrams, a premier Chicago law firm that specialized in derivatives. This certainly wasn't a firm of the bozos like before, and with a lot of hard work, my career started to take off. My parents were very proud of me, and I was too.

When I started, one of my first assignments was to draft a contract. I thought this should be a breeze having had a contracts class in law school. I finished the assignment in record time and then Liz was going to review it.

After a while, I started thinking, "Why is it taking her so long since she doesn't seem that busy right now?"

I met with Liz a few days later and she said that she had some comments. I thought okay, but there couldn't be many. I was surprised at how many there were. She wasn't mean or anything, but she was giving me good constructive criticism like a law firm supervisor should. She said that, in law school, they don't teach you how to write a contract, and she was right. I felt crushed since this was my first assignment and I didn't do it well.

Maybe I shouldn't have left my last job because it was safe there. I thought of calling them to see if they would take me back and to heck with this career progression thing. That old self-doubt that I had conquered was creeping back in again.

That night, walking home after work with tears in my eyes, it hit me. This is exactly what should be happening. I needed to learn to expand my legal skills and advance my career, and this was how it was going to happen.

My mind was made up. I wouldn't doubt myself and would try harder in the morning and every day after that without stopping. I would take the comments and not be hurt by them but use them to keep getting better as a lawyer. With this renewed confidence, I pictured myself as being a great lawyer.

If I didn't make any mistakes, I couldn't learn from them, so it was okay. If I kept picturing myself as a great lawyer, I would keep working to achieve it. I thought over and over. If you don't believe, you can't achieve.

Working with this new approach, the partners thought that I was doing good work, and everyone seemed to like me. The other important lesson that Liz taught me was about being an ethical lawyer and how important a reputation is. And my parents were always ethical too.

She taught me that, even in difficult circumstances, you have to stand your ground and be an ethical lawyer. I have carried that lesson with me to every job, and even when I could have lost some of my jobs for standing up for what I thought was right, I did it anyway.

After about six months at the law firm, it was time for my first performance review. I was nervous about it. The review was done by John, the one with the silver hair. I walked into his huge impressive office with traditional furniture, closed the door, then sat down across the desk from him.

We made some small talk, and John said that he was happy with my work and that they were glad that I was there. Whew, what a relief that was. And I was proud that my hard work was paying off. I expected our meeting to end there, but it didn't.

John then took the conversation in a different direction. You see, a few months after I had started at the firm, he started calling me "Eileen, my pet." I am not making this up as you just couldn't. His wife's name was also Eileen. There wasn't anything sinister about it, and he meant no harm. To him, it was a term of endearment and that he was taking me under his wing.

Every time I was working on something and met with John, he started the conversation with "Eileen, my pet." After each meeting, I would go to my floor and stop by Liz's office and tell her, and we would laugh so hard every time. We did it with the door closed just in case John came to the floor so we wouldn't get caught. It was always hysterical to us.

During my performance review, he also pulled the picture from the side of his desk and showed it to me. It was a nice picture of his family. I think he and his wife had around eight kids or some large number.

He said, "Eileen my pet, it is also important that you start to think about things in life other than work, like getting married and having a family."

He didn't just say that, did he?

This was during my first performance review at the fancy derivatives law firm.

"John, I appreciate this good review and your looking out for my future, but right now I'm focused on being the best lawyer possible. And with your help, I might get there."

"Don't let too much time go by, or you might regret it," John said.

I wasn't offended because he meant it sincerely and was looking out for me. It was a different time then and bosses could say things like that to employees.

Things at Franklin and Abrams were going well for me, and I even bought a fur coat from a low-end department store on an installment plan, making payments every month. It cost $1,200, and it took me two years to pay for it. I had a studio apartment, around thirteen navy-blue suits and a fur coat. I don't wear fur coats anymore, but that, too, was a different time, and a lot of people wore them back then. And I was so excited to be able to make the monthly payments on my own.

And then things changed rapidly and not for the better, for me or the law firm. I had heard that Franklin and Abrams didn't have a lot of legal business at the time, as they were very careful about the types of clients they represented. They always wanted to maintain their sterling reputation. It must have been true since one day, out of the blue, John announced to all of the lawyers at Franklin and Abrams that the firm was going to merge with another law firm.

The other group did insurance defense and not at all related to derivatives. I met with the other lawyers and their partners and I couldn't figure how this merger thing was going to work. The two groups had entirely different cultures and law practices. Pretty soon, it became clear to me that there was no way that this merger was going to work. The bickering and yelling didn't take long after the merger. And it seemed to take on more steam each week.

The other firm's lead partner, Craig Southport, wanted me to work for them doing insurance defense. I was loyal to my law firm partners but also thought that maybe some experience doing insurance defense could be good for my career.

I spoke to John and asked him, "Would you mind if I do some insurance defense work for the other group? Our firm's derivatives work will come first, and I'll fit in their work putting in extra hours and working over the weekends."

"Fine by me," he said.

I think that he didn't want to stand in the way of me getting more experience in the law. That was great of him, as he didn't have to go along with it.

Working for the other lawyers started out okay. I was working hard and getting everything done, but then they wanted more and more of my time. It was becoming obvious to me that I was another power play in this merger disaster and was nothing more than a pawn to the other new lawyers. Well, I wasn't going to be anyone's pawn and nobody fucks with a Flaherty, so I decided to find another job. I was worried, though, as it was starting to look like I'd had too many jobs in my short career. I had to get over that worry too.

As luck would have it, the timing was perfect because a large derivatives exchange in Chicago, the Chicago Exchange Markets, was looking for a junior attorney. I sent my resume to them, and they wanted me to come in for an interview. I wanted to get that job so much and went there to meet with some of their lawyers and the general counsel of the whole Exchange, Dan Randolph.

After a few days of waiting, Dan called and offered me the job and I accepted. I was going to be making $50,000 a year. I couldn't even believe it. I was sorry to leave Franklin and Abrams, but that whole merger thing was stressful on everyone, including a junior person like me. I didn't think it was ever going to work, and I was right.

About a year after I left, they did what never happens. They unmerged the two firms. But it was too late for me, and I was pretty sure that I never wanted to work for a law firm again. No more "Eileen, my pet." I still laugh at that.

CHAPTER TEN

A BIG JOB

I was thrilled to be joining the Chicago Exchange Markets and was becoming known in the industry as a derivatives lawyer. It was a first-class organization, but there were some not-so-first-class people there, although I didn't know it at the time.

The Exchange had a long history and had grown to become an internationally recognized company. Some people in the industry argued that it was the biggest derivatives exchange in the world, but there were enough of them claiming the same status, all using their own version of the statistics to support their claims.

The Exchange started out long ago with derivatives contracts on live cattle and hogs. Over the years, it grew to be a financial exchange with contracts on financial instruments and several of the largest stock indices. It was regulated by the Derivatives Trading Commission in Washington, DC, which was an important regulator in the federal government.

When I joined the Chicago Exchange Markets, there was a rival exchange a few blocks away, and the competitive spirits were sometimes hilarious—and they seemed to all be based on the egos of the people running the places.

One week, the exchange where I worked put up banners along Wabash Street saying they were the best exchange in the world. The next week, the other exchange would put up banners on that street that pretty much said the same thing. Eventually, the derivatives exchange where I worked swallowed up the other one and is now a division, not the big rival that it used to be.

There were some serious politics at the Exchange, but at that point in my career, I was too naïve to see them.

Thankfully, the women lawyers at the Exchange didn't have to wear navy-blue suits with white shirts and ties. That was real progress—that you could be a woman lawyer and not have to dress like a man. I stopped counting the number of my blue suits and was overjoyed to donate and get rid of all of them.

To this day, rarely do I wear blue or brown, as they remind me of the school uniforms I had to wear and the suits from my early days as a lawyer. Yuck.

I think I am color-scarred from all that uniform stuff. To get ready for my new job, I went out and bought some nice dresses to try and look very sharp.

On my first day of work, I was directed to my new office in an area where the other lawyers had their offices. Mine was awful. It was an internal office that was very dark and didn't have enough overhead lighting. I had heard that the lawyers were going to be moving to another floor and some of the offices had windows.

I vowed to move up the promotion chain as fast as I could to get out of that office. It was like a prison cell that had no energy. I met the other lawyers who worked there and again the general counsel, Dan, and they all seemed nice. I was also introduced to one of the most senior exchange officials, Chris Cabrini.

As luck, or at least I thought it was luck, would have it, his office was on the same floor and right around the corner from mine. I thought this was good placement for me, as maybe he would notice me more quickly and hopefully help to get me promoted. I was setting my sights pretty high. He seemed nice to me at that time, and I wish that I had known better.

I was given some general legal work from Dan, and I produced and turned it around at a quick clip. He recognized my work and thought that it was good. I always stayed late, even though the other lawyers didn't. I thought that was going to be another advantage for me, in terms of my plan of getting promotions.

The other junior lawyers came from fancier law schools than I did, but eventually I was promoted over all of them. And I thought I deserved it because of all my hard work and effort. None of them seemed to like me for that.

When I started at the Chicago Exchange Markets, nobody was specific about what I was going to be working on since their big secret project that nobody knew about had not yet been publicly announced. I was doing the junior legal stuff, and that was fine by me and it was interesting.

Then, within a few weeks, I was in a meeting with Dan, and he told me why they hired me.

"You're going to be the lead staff attorney working on the electronic trading system that we're developing and haven't announced to the public yet. It's going to be named Prime Markets Trading, and there will be a press release out soon," he said.

How amazing. I couldn't believe it.

"Thank you, Dan, this is a great opportunity for me, and I will work as hard as I can on it," I said.

I was over the moon excited about this. The announcement was going to be out soon, and this trading system was going to be the first one of its kind in the U.S. derivatives markets.

This job was going to be better than I ever thought.

After diving right into working on the project, the '87 market crash happened. The stock and derivatives markets were in a serious decline and weren't stopping. It was big. Billions of dollars were being lost by the hour, and some of the firms that did business in the derivatives markets were on the brink of financial collapse.

I was still a young lawyer, but the tension in the whole building was felt by everyone. The markets were melting down. It went on for days, and it seemed to get worse and worse. I was worried for the whole economy at the time. Senior executives at the Exchange were sleeping in their offices for days and working around the clock, but I didn't fully appreciate all of what was going on.

Chris asked if I would help him with something to prevent this mess from happening in the future. He wanted me to work on a rule, the first of its kind in the derivatives markets, that would act like a circuit breaker. If the markets dropped a lot, there would be a market halt and a break before trading could resume. It was supposed to be like a pause to give the markets and traders a bit of time to hopefully cool off.

"Do you think you can come up with a first draft of this new rule?" he asked me.

"Of course," I said to Chris even though I had no idea how to do it.

Since I wasn't experienced enough in trading to know what to do, panic set in. I worked around the clock to get myself up to speed to learn this stuff. It also didn't help that I was moving to a new apartment at the same time and that there was a short deadline for a draft of the rule.

I remember sitting on the floor, surrounded by moving boxes, and calling a friend asking, "How does this particular market thing work?" I had no idea, but it was critical to know to be able to draft this new and important rule. He helped me to understand, and luckily, I was able to come up with a first draft. It was okay, not great, but it was a start. Then things in the markets calmed down a bit and I got to go back to working on the Prime Markets Trading project again. That was a relief since I liked it and was getting a lot of notice from senior executives at the Exchange.

I had a significant level of responsibility for this project as the junior legal staff lead. Dan was also involved, but I did the work and had a seat at the table with the senior people at the Exchange. At this point in my career, to be on a team with these talented people, who were the best and brightest, was an honor. And I was going to prove myself and not let any one of them down. Applying my parents' work ethic, I usually worked six days a week and did my professional reading on Sundays.

Right before the first Christmas that I worked there, Dan called me into his office. Everyone in the department had a meeting with him that day. I had only been there a little less than three months. He said that they were very pleased with my work and that I was getting a bonus.

Dan explained that bonuses were based on an annual basis, so mine would be prorated to reflect the time that I had been there. It was $1,000, and I couldn't believe it. Having never worked at a place that gave bonuses, I was loving this place.

I told my parents, and they were so happy for me. They had never worked at any place that gave bonuses either. After learning about the bonus thing, I chased them over the many years of my career.

There were other lawyers who initially helped on the big project, but most of them dropped off and I was more than willing to take on the work.

Then I got my first promotion and my first raise. It was even a few thousand dollars, and that was huge to me. Eventually, I got to move to an office with a window and a view of the building across the street. I loved that office, and it was even better when I got promoted to be a vice president. That was a big deal since you got to work with a designer and pick out your own office furniture.

My style was very modern, so I picked a glass desk and a black leather couch and a coffee table too. To this day, that was still the best office ever, and I was always happy to be in it. I was also a chocoholic and kept a bottle of Hershey's syrup behind my desk and drank it straight when I needed a boost in the afternoons.

The harder I worked, more kept coming my way, and that was good for me. I was appreciated for my work and got another promotion with another raise. In recognition of all of my efforts, I was selected to represent the Exchange at a huge international conference for regulators and exchange representatives. It was going to be held in Tokyo, and I had never been there before. Working harder than ever and getting this opportunity was all that I could think about.

CHAPTER ELEVEN

TRIPS

Not knowing much about the Japanese culture at the time or what Tokyo was like, I thought it would be an eye-opener for me. And getting to fly business class made me feel like a queen. It was a long flight of about twelve hours. I wasn't used to that kind of travel, but it was exciting. Upon landing, I realized, Oh fuck, I forgot my business cards. They had been specially made with one side in English and the other side with my name and title in Japanese.

Who knew that business cards in Tokyo were such a big deal?

I learned at the conference that it is an important ceremony when a Japanese person gives you their card. They use two hands and present it to you. It is like they are presenting themselves. The other person in turn is supposed to do the same thing. Oh well, all I could say was that I forgot my cards. Ugh.

Meeting hundreds of people, I had to suffer this humiliation every time, but the trip was still good. It was the first time that I got to meet Japanese people and eat real sushi. I took a few hours to acquaint myself and went walking around the city. I thought it was dense, but the people seemed very friendly. It seemed safe too, so I felt okay walking around by myself even though I didn't speak any Japanese.

I learned during this trip how important honor and respect are in the Japanese culture and that came in handy in my future jobs. Their culture takes a long view, and I found that interesting. The focus isn't on making a quick buck; long-term relationships are worth far more.

Because of the Prime Markets Trading project, I also got to go to Paris to work on a deal with the French derivatives exchange, so the members of each exchange could trade the products of the other. I didn't know any more about the French culture than the Japanese before going to Tokyo, but I would have to figure it out. Once again, I flew business class, and this time to Paris.

For a kid from Burbank, this was as good as it gets.

I arrived at the hotel, and the general counsel was staying at the same one. We spent the entire week working with the people at their exchange, figuring out the details of the arrangement and how it would come together. It had never been done before, so it was interesting and fun.

I liked the people at the French exchange very much and stayed in touch with some of them long after the project had ended. Their English skills were impeccable, and it was a matter of pride with them. I remember, they took us to dinner at a fine restaurant named Jules Verne or something like that, and it was in the Eiffel Tower. I hadn't seen fine dining like that before, and the views of Paris were beyond anything in beauty—lucky me.

When the week ended, we had to go back to Chicago. I was sad to leave Paris and vowed to come back many times to appreciate its stunning history, culture, and beauty. That trip taught me so much about the French people and that, too, would come to help me later in my jobs.

Oh, and there was the trip to London too. There was an upcoming international conference, and I was the staff lawyer at the Exchange selected to go. One other woman at the Exchange, Lauren, had a senior role in the clearing of derivatives, which is how the money transfers for the trades, and she was selected to go too. We became good friends.

We started at the Exchange at about the same time, and it was clear that if we gals were going to succeed, we would need to support each other. Two other gal friends, Fran and Myra, were also in the derivatives industry and going to the same conference. I suggested that we all fly after the conference from London to Paris and spend the weekend there. After that, Fran and I would driving to the south of France, as neither of us had been there before. Everyone was totally psyched for the trip.

After the conference, the four of us flew to Paris and this was going to be a blast. Paris with three fun friends who all knew each other, and we all had a lot in common. Considering myself the Paris expert, I mapped out all of what we were going to do and see. My friends probably should not have trusted me with that responsibility. You see, I think you can only see Paris by walking, and we did, although there was a short boat trip down the Seine thrown in.

We arrived on Friday night after the conference and we were staying at the Grand Luxee Hotel, which was about a mile from the Eiffel Tower. We had two rooms for the four of us, so we shared the rooms to save expenses.

On Saturday morning we began the adventure.

"We'll walk to the Eiffel Tower and then over to the Arch de Triumphe, down the Champs Elysees, then to the Louvre. Next we'll see the Musee d'Orsay, and finally go to Notre Dame. Then we'll re-trace our way back and see everything one last time," I said.

They all nodded and were excited for the day of sightseeing in Paris.

We all appreciated every sight and, although exhausted, we didn't miss a thing. We did Paris in a day. When we got back to the Eiffel Tower, Fran, Lauren and Myra were literally laying on the grass unable to move.

I was fine.

We had a fun French dinner and then Lauren wanted to stay back from exhaustion, but Fran, Myra and I wanted to see a little more. We went to a bar where they had live French music. When we got back to the hotel, Lauren had fallen asleep and we didn't want to wake her up.

We had been out, let's say, a little too late at this point, so I said, "Don't worry, I will see if they have one of those roll out beds. That way Myra can stay in the room us." Fran and I were sharing.

It was late, but luckily a woman at the reception desk did answer the phone and, using my best French accent, although speaking English, I said, "Madam, we need le rollaway bed."

"Excuse me?" she asked in French. That was one of a handful of words I knew.

I said it louder, as if that would make her understand me better. She didn't. I had to try another route.

"Madam she is sick, she is ill," I said, all in my French accent.

The lady hung up the phone and came up to the room to figure out what was going on. Myra faked being sick, so we got le rollaway bed and stayed up even longer. That was a mistake and the morning came way too soon. We were all tired but agreed that we could not have had a better time. It was one of the best trips I have ever taken.

Fran and I got a rental car in Paris and started driving to the south of France. Thankfully she did all of the driving. We had a general sense of direction, but there weren't Google maps or anything like it at the time so it added to the adventure. We found a hotel which was a castle to stay at for a night. We also stopped in Burgundy at a bunch of wineries and kept sipping wine along the way.

The beauty of the French countryside was just so stunning. We went to Nice, although there was not much to see, and then to St. Tropez for lunch. Oh my god, the beaches and elegance, I didn't know places like this existed. Then we headed to Cannes for the next few days. I had made the hotel reservation, or I thought I had at a nice hotel on the French Rivera, thinking it would be so wonderful.

When we arrived in Cannes, all of the streets were blocked off and we couldn't get anywhere. Neither of us spoke French, and nobody understood my English with a French accent. We couldn't figure out what was going on or get to our hotel because it was blocked off for almost a mile and there was no way to drive there.

Fran rolled down the car window and there was a French lady walking by.

"Excuse me, do you speak English?" Fran asked.

"Yes," she said in a French accent.

We explained our dilemma that we 'had a reservation' and couldn't get into the hotel after trying for some time. She opened the back car door and jumped in and said,

"Let me help you."

"Please do," we said with some relief that someone actually understood us.

Her English was good and we were so grateful to meet this wonderful French woman.

Her name was Pauline and she was so much fun and so French. She told us where to drive, and we did as she said. Each time there was a roadblock she would get out of the car and speak with the armed guard and he would move the barricade to let us through. I couldn't believe we were making progress. We finally got near the hotel and she explained that there was some Middle

East summit going on in Cannes and most of the hotels had dignitaries staying there, so they were closed to the public.

Oh, this was going to be bad. Where would we stay?

And the trip had been going so well. Pauline got us to the hotel garage and explained to the guard that we had a reservation. He checked the trunk probably for bombs and then let us into the garage to park. We were immediately escorted straight to the reception area.

The hotel was nice but empty, except for a group of well-dressed what looked like men from the Middle East. I explained to the hotel reception guy.

"We have a reservation for three nights," I said using my best French accent.

"That is impossible the hotel is closed to the public," he said.

"Well, it wasn't closed to the public when I made the reservation," I said. I was insistent and firm although polite.

At that moment, I thought oh fuck I made the reservation for next week, but I had to stick to my story.

"Wait here," the hotel manager said and he walked away from the check-in desk.

As we were waiting I kept thinking, oh shit this is all my fault and we have no back-up plan.

After a long time, the hotel manager came to the desk and handed each of us a name badge. "You can stay for the three nights, but you each have to wear le badge at all times, to identify yourselves."

"That is fine with us," we said.

Le badge had to be worn everywhere. When someone stopped us, we said, "See le badge." And it worked.

Fran and I still laugh about le badge to this day. I didn't tell her for a long time that I had fucked up the reservation.

We were both sharing a room to save costs and I thought there was a good chance that our hotel room was bugged, in case we were not who we said we were. I also figured out that some security group had us followed everywhere we went. Each time Fran and I left the hotel and were out doing some sight-seeing, there was this drop-dead gorgeous guy in a light colored business suit that wasn't far away. He had dark hair and olive skin. He tried not to be obvious, but he was always there.

One morning I was up early and told Fran that I was going out running. Our room must have been bugged because when I went out of the hotel lobby, the gorgeous guy was right across the street watching me. I waved to him and pointed to the direction where I was going. We both smiled as his cover was busted. It would have been better for them if they had selected a frumpy old guy to follow us rather than the drop-dead gorgeous guy who definitely stood out.

I think our security detail finally figured out that we were not a threat; just two American gals who showed up when the hotel was closed. I didn't blame the hotel for being cautious, but was more worried for our safety, as what if someone did try to blow up the hotel with the dignitaries in it? I couldn't worry about it too much, since we had nowhere else to stay, and the trip was so much fun.

When the trip was over, it was time to get back to Chicago and back to work. I hadn't taken much vacation time as I was too busy with my big project at the time.

What I didn't know during my fun adventure was that there was something sinister going on behind my back, and that two people were planning what they thought would be my career demise.

CHAPTER TWELVE

DIDN'T SEE IT COMING

When I got back, my work was paying off and the Prime Markets Trading project was going well. There were also foreign regulatory approvals that I was working on and they were coming through too. I was hitting it on all parts.

I also did a lot of work getting the necessary regulatory approvals from the Derivatives Trading Commission in Washington DC and developing a good working relationship with the staff there. They were good, smart, and all worked hard and I would later come to work with some of these talented people again.

My visibility kept gaining within the exchange and the derivatives industry and I was also the lead legal staff attorney on several exchange committees, with members made up of important industry titans. It was kind of intimidating for me, because nothing that I had ever done prepared me for something this big. Like in sports, I had to act like I had been there before and that this was no big deal.

Based on my hard work I was also gaining in my own self confidence. I was even asked to give several presentations to the exchange board of directors, which was made up of more industry titans, who happened to be mostly men.

Some things never change.

I was getting invitations to speak at industry conferences and had to teach myself how to do public speaking and not be nervous—or at least not so nervous that people could see. I learned that if I held a pen when I was speaking, it was calming for me. Sometimes I still use it.

During this time, I also published industry articles and had totally come into my own in this job and was moving up the legal ranks each time. I would soon come to learn that a certain two people didn't like that.

There was one event that I will always remember. There were rumors at the time that there was some type of secret federal government sting operation on the trading floor of the Exchange. Nobody knew whether it was true or not.

Then it hit at the rival exchange; the U.S. Federal Bureau of Investigation—one scary group—had arrested several members who had traded on the rival exchange floor and charged them with violations of rules and laws. I felt bad for them, but I was also glad it happened at the other exchange and to nobody that I knew.

Then within a few days, early one the evening, I was in a conference room with Chris Cabrini, then his administrative assistant, Regina Court, came to the door looking panicked.

We immediately stopped working and she said, "Sorry to bother you, but Joe Roosevelt is on the phone and he said that he has a big problem."

Chris picked up the phone and listened and froze. Then he looked at me with panic on his face.

Chris put his hand over the phone and said, "The FBI just left Joe's house. They threatened to arrest him and take his house and car and other family possession. What should I tell him to do?"

I was very nervous, having never encountered anything like this before, and it was tense. I wasn't a seasoned lawyer with decades of experience, but I did my best to stay calm.

"Joe is in deep trouble and he needs to find a top white-collar criminal attorney. Maybe call Ryan Sacramento. He shouldn't use any general lawyers or cousins or friends; he has to get the best because he may be going to jail." I think it's one of the best answers I'd ever given.

Chris told Joe what I had said and they finished their conversation and he hung up.

"Thank you, I think that will help him," he said.

"This is big and bad, and there will probably be more traders implicated. This isn't the end of it," I said.

He nodded in agreement.

As this unfortunate drama unfolded, several more traders were arrested and charged with crimes as I expected. It was a long, drawn-out process, and I think that some of the people were innocent or committed minor infractions, but they got caught up in the whole thing.

What I also knew was that there were areas on the exchange floor that were thought to have a lot of trading violations, but they were too crowded with traders, so the FBI couldn't actually get to where the action might have been occurring.

Things were going well for me, although I had thought several times about whether I should leave the Exchange, to try and get some higher-powered position in the industry. I thought that staying too long at the Exchange might hurt my opportunities down the road. Nobody taught me that, but it made sense the more I thought about it. But I loved my job and maybe the next one might not be as good, so I stayed for seven-and-a-half years.

As I've mentioned earlier, the politics of the organization were lost on me, and that ended up hurting me. In large organizations, I now know that, as you rise up through the ranks, there is jealousy, backstabbing, and meanness for sport. I was in no way prepared for that, and wasn't looking for it or to be a participant.

What I didn't know was that Chris Cabrini had taken a liking to another guy lawyer, Mike Goethe, whom I didn't think was very smart or a good lawyer, so I didn't waste any time on him. They apparently became the duo as, one day, my world turned, and not in a good direction.

Chris and Mike planned to try to damage my career and for no good reason. They conspired behind my back when I was on my fun trip to London and Paris, but they must have been planning it for much longer. They arranged for the other senior lawyers to meet at a picnic at Mike's house to talk about me. I was never supposed to know about it.

They all met there so Mike could try to get dirt on me and get the other lawyers to say that they didn't like me. It had all been set up. Of course, they didn't like me. I had been promoted over every one of them because of my hard work.

As luck would have it, there was an administrative assistant, Barbara Lake, who had integrity. She had heard about the picnic and its purpose and didn't like it one bit. At great risk to her own job, Barbara told me what they had done. I was grateful to her and for her character. There wasn't much that I could do, so I kept going and forgot about it.

Having worked my way up to be the second-highest lawyer at the Exchange, reporting directly to Dan, the general counsel, I had other lawyers reporting to me. Then one day, Chris called me into his office. His tone was serious.

"I've made the decision to remove your management responsibilities from you. I'm promoting Mike. You'll be reporting to him from now on," he said.

This asshole was demoting me.

How could he be saying this? I worked harder and delivered more work than he and the others did, and everyone knew that.

They had conspired behind my back.

While he was saying this, it took everything inside me not to react.

"I want you to stay at the Exchange because we value your legal talents," Chris said.

What an asshole thing to say.

"In ten minutes, I'm holding a meeting with the whole legal department to announce the changes and I expect you to be there," he said.

Not knowing what to do, I called my good friend, Carol, and she immediately said, "Fuck him. Don't go to that meeting. You will be humiliated."

She was right, so I didn't go.

Fuck him.

I was stunned, and the range of emotions were broad. I had worked so hard to get those promotions, and now those two were taking something away from me without any warning. The job with all of the responsibilities that I had loved and earned was gone, and this place would never be the same for me again.

I was numb for about an hour and then got my strength back. Nobody fucks with a Flaherty. And I reminded myself that fortune does favor the bold. Chris said that he wanted me to stay at the Exchange, so screw him. I was getting out no matter what.

For the next few days, I worked the phones calling all of the titans that I had come to know and said that I wanted to leave the Exchange and asked if they would keep me in mind if they heard about any legal positions. And they did.

I had an interview scheduled with one of the biggest firms in New York for a prestigious job, and then I got an offer from a firm based in Chicago headed by Leon Clark, an important figure in the derivatives industry. He offered me my first general counsel job.

Weighing the two options, I knew there wasn't much time to decide. I wanted to show those two assholes that I could get a big job in six weeks or less. Later in my career, I learned that that time frame was nearly impossible, and it was good that I didn't know it at the time. After thinking about it, I wasn't ready to move to New York, so I accepted the big job in Chicago. I was going to be the general counsel for a prominent firm in the industry headed by Leon Clark.

I gave my two weeks' notice and was gone before Chris had come back from a vacation. I heard that he was surprised that I had left. What an asshole.

My job was over and there was no looking back. It is too difficult in those situations to see the future and how it all works out, but it does. I had stayed in my job for seven-and-a-half years, and that was probably too long. Maybe I should have taken a risk sooner and left, although it wasn't clear to me at the time.

And it did work out. I went on to make more money and have an exciting career traveling the world, and none of it would have happened if I had stayed at that job. Thanks, Chris.

It is always disappointing to me that the old saying "what goes around comes around" never seems to happen that way. Or, at least if it does happen, you may not know about it to revel in it.

Well, thankfully, this time it was different. Chris kept getting his fair-haired boy Mike promoted on the business side until one day Mike made it to the top position. And then Chris was gone. Unseated by Mike, I'm pretty sure. I think what happened was that Mike used Chris to get to the top, and then he didn't need him anymore. It is a beautiful day when something goes and comes around and you are actually able to hear about it. This time I did.

And what made this even better is that, after Mike rose up through the ranks to the top position, one day he was gone. Unseated. Ha again. A good ending, in my opinion.

The organization is more prominent than ever now.

CHAPTER THIRTEEN
THE FINANCIAL FIRM AND
THE JAPANESE

It was going to be so cool to have my first general counsel job. I had left that last job, having found this new one in record time. There was a sense of pride having made it to this level in my career. My parents were so proud too.

The financial services firm where I was going to work was a subsidiary of the Industrial Bank located in Japan. The subsidiary company's offices were located in the very same building as my last job, which wasn't so great, but I still had the strength to ignore those assholes who had tried to sabotage me and failed. My new firm wasn't huge, but it had a very good reputation. The whole derivatives industry had heard about my new job before I even started telling people.

Before leaving my last job, I had gotten a call from another industry titan, Gary Bell, who was a wonderful and super nice guy. He was calling to give me a heads-up about some politics at my new job.

Oh no, not again.

"Watch out for one of the very senior gals there, Sharon Claremont, because she might have it out for you," Gary said.

"Thank you so much, Gary. It was considerate of you to think to tell me," I said, grateful for that tip. I didn't ask him how he knew. Gary was a connected guy, and if he was telling me something, it was true.

Why would she have it out for me? I didn't even know her.

I had heard Sharon's name a few times, but I didn't think she had a big reputation or anything. I was going to do my best to steer clear of her, but within days of starting my new job, I realized that that wasn't going to be easy.

The firm was owned by a Japanese bank, and I thought that understanding more about their culture before starting would be good, so I bought two books. That proved to be a good move, and it was well worth reading them ahead of time. One book was about how the Japanese do business, cherish their reputations, and take a long view. It was very helpful.

The second book was about non-Japanese women doing business with Japanese men. It talked about how, in the Japanese culture, women can be marginalized. They can be the smartest people in the room, but they rarely get noticed. It also talked about where to sit in a conference room to create an impression of power. If you didn't do it the right way in the beginning, you wouldn't get a second chance. It was all good advice that I relied on as soon as I got to my new firm.

My office at the new job was nice, not as cool as my last office with the black leather furniture, but it was definitely a general counsel's office. I was the only lawyer at the firm and very early on was introduced to the two Japanese guys who were stationed at the firm to watch out for the bank's investment. They were very nice to me, and I immediately applied my new skills of dealing with Japanese businessmen.

They had an assistant, Utami, who was Japanese, and she had been in the United States for many years. I learned how educated and smart she was. Unfortunately for her, because she was a Japanese woman, part of her job was to wait on them and get their coffee and stuff like that. I thought that was too bad, but she didn't seem to mind, as she knew their culture.

The Japanese men seemed to respect my skills. They didn't second-guess my opinions and followed my advice. I was a member of the board of directors of the company and they seemed glad that I had that position too.

I was working hard and enjoying my new job and liked most of the people there, except for that Sharon. It was abundantly clear to me early on that she did have it out for me, and Gary had been right, of course, about Sharon gunning for me. She was so rude to me. She would give me mean looks if she walked past. She didn't say hello, and the few times when she did, it was cold.

I thought that she was a bitch.

I tried being nice to Sharon in the beginning and went out of my way. I ditched that approach when it became clear that she wanted no part of me. And then one day, she left the firm. I wasn't sure but maybe she had gone to Leon and said it was her or me that had to go. I never did anything to her to deserve that.

The bitch was gone.

It was great working with the compliance team, which consisted of Carrie Wells and Jemma Bell, who were two nice and smart gals. The other people there were great too. Leon, the head of the firm, respected me and my work, so my efforts were paying off. It was a nice place to work and I was still learning, but there weren't any fun international trips with this job, so I started to wonder about maybe finding a job at a bigger firm.

After about a year and a half of being there, I had learned the Japanese culture, more derivatives law, and a little bit of securities law too. There were contracts to review and human resources issues to deal with from a legal perspective. But I was getting a bit restless and decided I should be making some more career progress. I was never satisfied to just have a nice job that I liked, and I kept taking chances in order to advance my career.

One day, I got a call from a guy named Tom Liberty, who was the chief operating officer at a boutique Wall Street securities and derivatives firm, Lange and Anderson.

They had decided to hire their first general counsel, and he asked me, "Are you interested in interviewing for the job?"

The job was in New York, so I wasn't sure that I wanted to do that. When a New York offer had come before, I wasn't ready to move there, but I told him, "Sure, I'd be interested in interviewing for the job."

Within a few days, I flew to New York for the interview. Their offices were in lower Manhattan, three blocks away from the World Trade Center. While waiting in their reception area, I was so impressed by the Persian rugs and antique furniture everywhere. It all screamed money.

A kid from Burbank in this office, interviewing for the general counsel position. Wow.

I was sure that I wasn't going to get the job because this whole thing seemed out of my league.

The first meeting was with Tom, then the president, Joe Waters, and also the chairman of the board of the company, Jerry Nassau. Each of them seemed impressed with my background, which surprised me since I didn't think that I was qualified yet to be a Wall Street general counsel.

The whole place was so gorgeous that I must have looked like some bumpkin, as my jaw kept dropping. I had never seen anything like this and thought, "So this is what Wall Street looks like." They showed me the trading room where a lot of activity was going on. There were people yelling from one side of the room to the other. And it was filled with men and women who were very impressive.

They had a dining room with more fancy rugs and historical pictures of the firm. The view was unbelievable. It was on the 49th floor of Two Chase Manhattan Tower, and they had the whole floor. You could see all views of Manhattan, from downtown to uptown. I didn't want to get too excited thinking it wasn't likely they were going to hire me.

The next day, I was back in Chicago as if nothing had happened. I had called in sick to fly out to New York for the interview. I couldn't tell anyone that I was going to interview for another job or risk getting fired for that.

A few days later, Tom called.

"We'd like to offer you the job to be the general counsel of Lange and Anderson, and we hope that you'll accept and join us."

I was shocked.

Then he told me how much they were going to pay me as a base salary and guaranteed bonus for the first year and I nearly dropped the phone. I didn't know how Wall Street worked, but that the bonus could end up being as much as half your salary and eventually maybe more. Companies in Chicago didn't pay bonuses like that, and I remembered being so grateful for the $1,000 bonus at the Exchange.

"I'm very interested and will get back to you with an answer in a day or two."

"Good. We'd be thrilled to have you as our general counsel," he said.

I walked home that night and thought about it. I needed to talk to my mom for her opinion. When I went to New York to the training program for the stock brokerage firm, I remember thinking that someday I should get back there, but I wasn't sure that this was the right time for me. It didn't feel right.

I thought, on the other hand, it would be a gigantic step for my career to be a general counsel on Wall Street.

My mom and dad were so proud and excited, but they left the decision to me. I gave them a lot of credit for that because I knew that they didn't want me to move and they had heard that New York was dangerous. But they also didn't want me to miss a chance if it would be good for me and my career. I thought and thought and got back to Tom a few days later, accepting the job. I was going to be the general counsel of Lange and Anderson, and I was moving to New York. Wow.

I told Leon that I was going to take a job in New York. He then offered me a salary increase to stay. He didn't want me to leave and I was glad about that, having so much respect for him. I told him that it wasn't about him or his firm, but about trying out New York and doing more securities work in addition to my derivatives work. I came to learn later that I would be doing a lot more than that.

Leon understood and there was a nice going-away party for me. I said my goodbyes, knowing many of these colleagues would be at industry events and we could keep in touch. I was glad to have had that opportunity to work there.

There was so much to do before moving to New York. I decided to rent an apartment there and keep my condo in Chicago, not knowing if I wanted to be in New York permanently. I wanted to hedge my bets on that one. I had to pack and get totally organized, operating on adrenaline.

When everything was packed in my condo and ready to go, all of a sudden I was sad. My mom was there helping me, and I started to cry.

"What is wrong?" she asked me.

"I don't want to go. I don't want to move," I said.

But it was too late. I had made the commitment, some stuff had already been moved, and there was no going back. I told myself that this move would be for two years and then I would come back. I kept reminding myself that fortune favors the bold. I felt better knowing that this wasn't going to be permanent. It would be like serving a short sentence, and then I would be free to come back to Chicago.

CHAPTER FOURTEEN
MADE IT TO NEW YORK

I arrived in New York the weekend before starting my new job. I was staying at a furnished apartment on the Upper East Side of New York, which was paid for by my new company. It was a very nice two-bedroom in a midsized building on the Upper East Side of Manhattan. I had three months to find my own apartment and move. I walked around by myself and got the lay of the neighborhood—where the grocery store was and what else was around. There was a lot to prepare for my first day as a Wall Street general counsel, and it was exciting.

Thankfully, my temporary boxes that had been sent ahead had arrived, and I had to unpack my business clothes, gym wear, and stuff that would get me through the first few months. On Sunday morning, I decided to do a dry run of how to take the subway downtown to where the office was. It took me a little while to figure out the underground system—which stops were near the office, and the best one that was the closest.

I immediately didn't like the subway system. It was dark in the tunnels waiting for the trains. At the stop on 57th where I got on, you had to take multiple levels of escalators down to go underground. It felt creepy, but it was the only efficient way to get around Manhattan.

Arriving at the Wall Street stop, I walked to the office building, which was about a block away. The building was huge with some sort of white marble stone on the plaza leading into the building. It was amazing. I wasn't going in or anything since it was closed, but I couldn't get over how impressive this new office thing was going to be. I walked around the area, which was very quiet on a Sunday, and became familiar enough that Monday's commute would be okay.

I got back on the subway and headed to my temporary apartment. I had a quiet evening and got everything ready for my first big day. My apartment building had a gym, so I worked out there that morning and left in plenty of time to get to the office early. I was so early that I waited in the receptionist area of the firm until the receptionist arrived.

The firm occupied the whole 49th floor of the building, and it was even more beautiful than I had remembered from the day that I came in for the interview. The views were stunning. There was a main hall that had large formal framed pictures of the prior chairmen of the firm since its inception in the 1950s.

The executive offices were all huge, with Wall Street–type wood furniture. The trading room was large with different trading desks, which I would later come to understand much better. There were the operations and technology areas, which pretty much kept the firm running. Everyone seemed nice to me.

The firm was well established and respected on Wall Street. I learned that being a Wall Street firm didn't necessarily mean that the offices were on Wall Street. The term was used to identify important financial firms in New York. My new firm was not huge in size, but it was in trading and its positions in the market, and I would come to learn a lot more about that too. It was an American company owned by a French bank, so I could use the skills that I had learned when I worked with the people in Paris from the French derivatives exchange.

After being escorted to my new office, I noticed that the furniture was like the others. The room was big with unbelievable views, so I was pretty sure I was going to like this place. Tom, who was the chief operating officer, stopped by to give me the lay of the land and help me settle in. He told me they served breakfast and lunch. They actually had an on-premises chef, Laurie Hudson.

Breakfast was simple, but the lunches were more like a full dinner. Laurie was very talented and passionate about the quality of her creations, and she was fun.

I was given the full tour of the trading floor and introduced myself to the traders, sales teams, and all of the executives. The chief financial officer was a woman named Holly Broadway, and I was sure that I was going to like her.

Over time, we ended up having to get through a bunch of sticky stuff together, and we made a good team.

The first day was a blur. I was their first general counsel, and I was certainly on center stage and not from New York. I was a kid from Burbank who was now a Wall Street lawyer. I couldn't let on what a big deal I thought this was or I would stick out like some unsophisticated Midwesterner.

The second day was exhausting too, and I was glad to see it to an end. I did note that they had a small gym in the office and separate shower rooms for the men and women. I decided to work out there in the mornings, since it would be more efficient, but I would have to leave home much earlier. I left the next day with my work and workout clothes and set out for the subway. It was dark and the streets were empty. I kept looking over my shoulder to make sure I was not being followed.

I settled into a daily routine at the office and got to know all of the people. The receptionist, Judy East, was polite and friendly, and the food was oh so good. The traders, who were mostly men, were all respectful. It was clear that nobody wanted to break any regulatory rules or get into trouble because they would ask and discuss a rule so they could understand. I was always walking through the trading floor, making myself accessible to the traders, and they seemed to appreciate it.

Not only was I the general counsel, I was also the corporate secretary. Being their first general counsel, I helped define the role and all that needed to be done. I made lists of what a general counsel is responsible for, and the executives were amazed at all that may have been missed without that role.

There was lots of legal work to get done like contracts and giving my opinions on the regulations of the markets and how to stay out of trouble. A firm like Lange and Anderson must follow the rules of the banking, securities, and derivatives regulators. And there were a lot of rules. Initially, I didn't have responsibility for the compliance function, which reviews trades and ongoing surveillance of the firm's activities. After about a year, I was also given the responsibility for compliance when people realized that I had that background too, and I hired a guy to help me.

I attended the board meetings as the general counsel and corporate secretary, but I started to note a common theme early on. The firm wasn't making money. Their primary regulator was the Federal Research Bank.

Lange and Anderson had wanted to expand their business to generate revenue in some simple and non-risky ways and needed the Fed's approval to do it. At the time, it seemed to me that the Fed hated the banks from France and their affiliates and had unlimited authority to stall any approvals. And that they did, which meant more board meetings and more money lost.

I was the first general counsel for the company and worked hard to earn the respect of the executives and everyone. At this point in my career, I also didn't back down or take anything from anyone, including the executives. Nobody fucks with a Flaherty.

I was taught early on in my legal career, by my friend Liz, to be an ethical and compliance-minded lawyer, and I always kept true to that. I also thought that, if you looked weak, the executives would think you were weak, and I couldn't have that either. Wall Street was male dominated, and as a woman who was the general counsel, I had to play nice. But that didn't mean I had to take any shit from anyone. I was glad that I was a Flaherty and had come a long way in building my confidence to that point.

I hated the subways, especially the stop at 57th, because there were too many levels to get underground to the trains. I even saw people living in the tunnels. There was one good thing about it, though—I made a friend, and I will always be grateful for how he helped me.

He got to the 57th stop early in the mornings like me, and we started talking to each other. It was just hello at first, as this was New York, and New Yorkers can be cautious. After we got to know each other better, he told me his name was Philip. He told me about his family and job, and I talked about being from Chicago and my new job.

In the mornings, I always wore my workout shorts to save time until one day Philip said, "Don't wear shorts on the subway and get sweatpants right away. You don't want to be noticed down here. There's all kinds of people in New York."

Another reminder of all the things I didn't know about living in the Big Apple.

"Thanks, Philip." What else could I say? I went out right after work and bought myself sweatpants and never wore my workout shorts on the subway again.

"Be safe," he said.

One day, I just stopped seeing him, and even though we only ever saw each other on the subway, I hoped that he and his family were okay. I still think of him as Subway Philip, and I often wonder if I would have made it safely without his sage advice.

Within three months of being in New York, I found an apartment on the Upper West Side. It was a brand-new building. I signed a two-year lease and had the other apartment for an extra week to move when I could.

I had heard about some older buildings there having roaches and I didn't want any of that. It was a one-bedroom apartment in a tall high-rise with a sliver of a view of Central Park, and the neighborhood seemed good. It was right around Columbus Circle, which was even better because the subway was close by.

This subway stop was brighter, so I was more optimistic. I arranged for the moving company to move my furniture, which had been in temporary storage, to my new building. There would have to be multiple trips from the east side of Manhattan from my temporary apartment to the west side to move my clothes and three months of stuff, which had grown substantially. The problem was that my temporary apartment was too close to Bloomingdale's.

With the whole week to move, although I was working, I thought that it should all work out. On Sunday, around midday, I put the first load of boxes in the taxi, and we proceeded to try to get to the new apartment, which was about a mile away. The taxi was moving, and then suddenly, it was a dead stop in heavy traffic and we couldn't get anywhere.

Fuck.

I didn't understand that since it was the weekend and traffic was usually lighter.

"What's the problem?" I asked the driver.

"Oh, it's the Puerto Rican Day Parade," he answered matter-of-factly.

"So why are we stopped?"

"To get to the West Side, we have to cross Fifth Avenue, and that's where the parade is. The police let one car go through at a time between the floats."

Well. Fuck.

I wasn't familiar with that, but apparently the Puerto Rican Day Parade is a big deal in New York. I think it was one of my most expensive taxi rides ever, but the driver seemed pretty pleased with himself. Of course, he had to have known this was going to happen. I got the rest of the stuff the next Saturday, since I wasn't going to be a sucker again. There are so many hard lessons that nobody tells you about New York.

It was a few months into the job and things were going well, except for that losing money thing at the firm. I had gained more respect from the people there because of my work ethic that I think they eventually forgot that I wasn't from New York. Some New Yorkers can be snooty that way to outsiders. And although I know my parents missed me, they were proud of their daughter on Wall Street. They even came for a few days to visit me and went to see the wonders of New York and Ellis Island.

Soon, the firm's Christmas party was coming up, and then I was going home for Christmas. The party was to be held at a fancy venue, but I was a little surprised that it was on a Saturday night and no spouses were allowed. Still, I was looking forward to my first extravagant New York party. Early in the evening, I was talking to a few people and enjoying the pleasant holiday vibe when Joe came up to us with a basket of nuts and a nutcracker.

"Who wants one?" he asked.

"No, thanks," I said. "Those are way too hard to open."

I should have known that something was up when the others jumped in to take theirs. When the nut was cracked open, a condom fell out of each.

My jaw dropped. Oh. My. God. Did that happen? What should I do now?

I knew that it was meant as a joke and nothing more sinister, but it was totally inappropriate. I was torn between leaving the party and staying after that, but if I left, I wouldn't know what happened, so I decided to stay and observe. I needed to make sure that nothing more tasteless happened. It was not a fun party after that.

It bothered me all weekend thinking about what I should do. It was a joke and it was a party, and I am not some sensitive prude, but as the general counsel, it was my obligation to look out for the firm.

Some of the other women at the party didn't think it was funny either and came to my office first thing Monday morning to let me know. I decided to do something about it. I was worried about losing my job with the new expensive apartment and everything. But I couldn't let that stop me. Addressing the issue was the right thing to do.

The following Monday morning, I called Joe.

"When you have a moment, would you mind stopping by my office?"

"I can be there in a few minutes," he said.

When he arrived, I closed the door.

"What were you thinking, doing that at the party?"

I'd only been at Lange and Anderson for about nine months and he was more senior than I was. Joe could fire me. I didn't care, though, and felt compelled to have a serious conversation with him.

"It was a joke," he said.

"Maybe, but some of the women were offended by it, and that is a problem," I said.

He didn't say anything else and left my office and looked agitated, but I had no regrets. Whatever was going to happen would happen.

To his credit, later that day, Joe came to my office and said he had thought about it and he agreed with me. I am not sure if we ever liked each other after that, or maybe he never liked me to begin with. But I didn't regret what I had done.

"What should I do to address the issue?" he asked me.

I said, "What's done is done, but next year, spouses need to be invited to the party."

I thought that surely the atmosphere would be different with spouses there. The next year, spouses came to the Christmas party, and of course, many of the men complained that the party wasn't as much fun anymore. I wasn't a bit sorry about that either.

CHAPTER FIFTEEN

FUNG SHWAY

My career kept moving along at Lange and Anderson, except for that losing money thing. The financial part was not my area, so I stayed out of it, but I was always curious as to why the firm was losing money. I thought that maybe if we cut some costs and had fewer fancy parties, that would be a good place to start, but nobody wanted to do that.

Then one day, to my surprise, Tom stopped by my office to let me know that we were going to have a fung shway guy come to the office. He was supposed to be a fung shway expert and was coming to find out if there was a problem with the offices, which maybe could have something to do with why the firm was losing money. I had heard a little of fung shway before, like if you walk into an entryway and there is a wall, there should be a mirror. It has to do with the feel of a space, or if it is jinxed, or something like that.

Tom was letting me know because the guy was going to stop by each executive office, including mine, and the entire space of the firm.

"Tom, you can't be serious," I laughed. I couldn't believe that we were resorting to fung shway to see if the firm was jinxed to solve the losing money problem.

He shook his head. "It's someone else's idea."

I had not seen any of this in my jobs in Chicago and thought that maybe it was a New York thing, as some New Yorkers can be different.

On the fung shway day, I stayed in my office thinking that the whole thing was hysterical, but I didn't want to offend the guy by laughing at his serious work. He was getting paid to do this, after all. I don't even know how they found the fung shway guy and didn't want to ask. When it was my turn to have the guy come into my office, Tom walked Mr. Fung Shway to the door.

He was an exotic-looking, petite Asian man, wearing black leather pants and a green silk shirt. Not knowing any better, I guessed that you had to dress like that if you are claiming to be a fung shway expert.

"Hello," I said.

He didn't say anything and looked out the windows. My office had large views of Manhattan, so he seemed to be pleased with my space. I could tell from his expression that he didn't think my office was jinxed, and I didn't either.

Before he left my office, I asked him a question.

"I've always been interested in whether my birthday was good luck in terms of Chinese numerology." I didn't believe in any of this, but he was there, so I asked him. "My birth date is unique, as the numbers repeat and reverse themselves."

"What is the date?" he asked.

"January 16, 1961," I told him.

His expression immediately changed. I could tell by the look on his face that something was wrong. He went from being happy in my office to someone who looked more serious.

"What time of day were you born?" he asked.

"I think in the middle of the night."

His expression got even worse, and he backed out of the doorway, raced down the hall mumbling something, and never came back to my office.

Years later, I was still curious about the answer to that question, so when I was in Hong Kong, I asked a colleague and good friend of mine, Linda Queensway, if my birthday with the repeating reverse numbers was lucky or unlucky in Chinese numerology.

She laughed at me and said, "Well, technically it's not lucky, but nobody believes in that stuff anymore. Don't worry about it." She added a moment later, "In Europe, your repeating numbers are considered lucky."

Since I'm Irish, I decided that she was right, and I should go with the European approach. I am lucky, even if the weird Asian guy went running down the hall away from me.

Mr. Fung Shway came back to Tom a few days later with the results from the fung shway day, and they were not good. It seemed that, according to him, one of the offices was jinxed. It was the largest corner one occupied by the CEO, Joe Wacker. It was beautiful, with expensive furniture and great views of downtown Manhattan.

That corner office was adjacent to the JP Morgan building on Wall Street, and you could see a lot of it. Apparently, that was the problem. The building was taller than ours, so I guess it was looking down at our building and that corner office in particular, making it the bad-luck office. Seriously, I couldn't believe any of this.

Well, to my surprise, people took this stuff very seriously, and Joe moved out of his office. That beautiful one still had the furniture in it, but nobody was going to occupy it. I volunteered to take it, but they didn't want anyone in there letting the bad luck seep out. The next CEO didn't use that office either.

That corner office stayed vacant until a few years later when the head guy leading the merger of the U.S. subsidiaries of three French banks was stationed in our space. He was the spy guy, so we wanted him in the jinxed office. Of course, we didn't tell him that it was jinxed. He was so proud to have the biggest office and moved right in. At that point, I was hoping that all of that fung shway stuff were true and that it was jinxed. We wished him the very best in that office and all that it had to offer. More about him later.

Sometime later, I learned that fung shway is actually spelled feng shui.

Oops.

CHAPTER SIXTEEN
ROCKET MAN

I had to learn several additional areas of law to be able to do the job, like foreign exchange trading and precious metals, and that was manageable, but there were some other things that I wasn't prepared for. There were the fire drills, not literally, and other events where thinking on my feet was required, and fast when I hadn't encountered the certain situation before.

There were no other lawyers at the firm, so it was just me and my one compliance guy. There were days when I was leaving the office and it felt like my hair had been on fire from the first thing in the morning until I left the office. One, which I later called NASA day, seemed like something right out of a spy movie.

It became obvious to me that there was a problem at the firm when one of the gals who worked there came running down the hall and burst into my office, motioning for me to stop what I was doing or get off the phone. One morning, that is precisely what happened.

"You've got to get to the reception area and there's no time to explain," she said, completely out of breath.

When I got there, Judy, the receptionist, was sitting at her post and looked panicked. "He's walking down the hall toward the research area."

I wanted to ask her who, but I realized I couldn't wait around to hear her answer, since it was clear that something was wrong.

I raced after the guy. Lang and Anderson had a very prominent presence in research in the financial markets and he was about to walk right into the research area.

I stopped him and said, "I'm Eileen Flaherty, the general counsel of this firm. And who are you?"

I acted fast and escorted him into the large internal conference room with glass windows, which we called "the fishbowl." I knew that I needed to isolate him to find out what was going on, as I had no information at that point.

The fishbowl was the room used for internal meetings and arguments. You weren't allowed to raise voices in the trading room, except when making trades. When someone had a beef with another person, they went into the fishbowl. Everyone could see them screaming at each other and, although you couldn't hear, it was pretty obviously when people were fighting.

Following the man into the fishbowl, I closed the door,

"Take a seat."

He did and handed me his card. Before I had a chance to look at it, he said, "I'm from NASA."

"The National Association of State Securities Administrators," I said and was instantly on guard. They coordinated the state regulation of financial firms.

What could the firm have done wrong? Why was he here? Why was he by himself? Regulators rarely roll alone, and they always come in wolf packs.

"No, I'm from NASA," he said again.

I finally got a good look at his card and, to my complete surprise, it said NASA.

"You mean like the Cape Canaveral people?" I am no space expert, but I knew from the news where NASA was generally located.

"That's right." His card didn't say Cape Canaveral; it said another location, and it wasn't in Florida. I had to try to think smart and fast.

"I wasn't expecting any visitors and have a conference call that's starting in a few minutes. I can't miss it." Of course, that was a load of bull. "It shouldn't take more than thirty minutes and then I'll be back."

After leaving the fishbowl, I had one of the research gals stand outside the door.

"Make sure he doesn't try to get out and wander anywhere."

"I'm on it," she said.

Oh shit, what was I supposed to do now?

My brain raced as I headed back to my office, walking calmly and pretending nothing was wrong. I had his card in my hand and my first instinct was to make sure this guy was not a fraud or an imposter. That seemed far more likely than NASA visiting our Wall Street firm; we had nothing to do with space. We didn't trade in space company stocks or anything like that, so I couldn't imagine any connection between our firm and NASA.

I found the general number for NASA at that location. Interesting. I asked for the human resources department and finally got through to someone. I realized in the same moment that there was no way he could have arranged all of that, but I was still at a loss as to why this person was here.

"I need to verify the identity of someone who is claiming to be a NASA employee and showed up at our offices unannounced." I read his name and title from the card, and the woman put me on hold.

It wasn't long before she was back, but all she would say was, "Yes, he's an employee of NASA."

I suppose that was good news, but I was still at a loss as I headed back to the fishbowl. I'm fairly certain that he knew what I'd been up to, but I don't regret my decision. I hadn't been faced with that situation before, and I'm glad to say I have never had one like that again.

What he said next almost had me laughing hysterically, even more than the fung shway guy, as there was no way that it could be true.

He said, "NASA has identified several financial firms in Lower Manhattan and specific computers that were used to attempt to hack into NASA's computers." This was in the early nineties, when hacking wasn't as widespread as it is today. "NASA has identified a particular computer at your firm."

This computer was assigned to Larry Rector, in the research area of our firm.

I didn't know Larry well, but I couldn't imagine that it was true. I was about to say that there wasn't anyone here who was smart enough to do what he was suggesting, and sign an affidavit that said so, but I didn't.

Instead, I said, "Haven't you people heard of firewalls?"

"You'd be amazed. I need to speak with the individual who uses that computer," he said.

"Do you have a written request or a subpoena," I asked.

"No, but a quick conversation might clear it up very easily," he said.

That is always a lie. The Feds lie a lot about stuff like that.

"Wait here, and I'll discuss it with that employee."

I approached Larry and explained that a guy from NASA was in the conference room saying something about a hacking and that it all seemed very farfetched. He looked more nervous than he should have, since he should have been laughing with me and he wasn't.

"This guy from NASA wants to talk to you. He doesn't have a subpoena and you have the choice to speak with him or not." I gave Larry some advice. "As the general counsel, I represent the firm and not you, but if there is any reason that you should not talk to this guy, then you might want to consider declining."

Larry agreed to speak with the NASA guy and asked if I would be in the room.

"Yes, but just as an observer if you want me there."

He sure did. The questions were direct.

"How long have you been with Lange and Anderson?"

"How long have you lived in New York? "

"What is your position here?"

"Have you been working with computers long?"

"Any experience programming?"

And then he asked the real reason for the visit.

"Did you, or anyone you know, ever attempt to hack into NASA's computers?" It was very direct.

Larry should have been laughing or smiling, but he wasn't.

He gave short answers and said no to the last. His answers seemed to lack conviction.

The NASA guy packed up, saying that he might be back. As we left the fishbowl, Larry thanked me for being there.

As I walked back to my office, I remembered something from when I started my new job. For the first few weeks, the computer in my office was not getting a consistent internet connection. The technology guys kept trying to fix it, but that was taking too long. I had work to do and asked if I could use one of the computers in the research area. They all left the offices earlier than I did every day, so I could use one after they left. It seemed like a simple request that wouldn't bother anyone.

The technology guys said that it would be fine so long as the research people were okay with it. I went to the research area and explained the internet problems and asked if I could use one of their computers after they left for the day. I said that it wouldn't disturb anyone during the day.

Larry stood up from his desk and yelled, "There is no way you're going to use any of our computers."

He was adamant and it was a bit scary but also very odd since nobody else seemed to care.

I left and went to the technology guys insisting that they speed up fixing my internet connection because finding another computer wasn't worth the drama. But looking back, maybe there actually was someone smart enough there to do that NASA hacking attempt thing.

A few years later, someone was making death threats to the former president of the firm. I heard that Larry was arrested for it and sentenced to some time in prison. I thought that guy was more dangerous than I ever knew.

CHAPTER SEVENTEEN

THE RUSSIANS

I liked most of the people at Lange and Anderson, although not Larry after the NASA day with rocket man. The trading and sales groups weren't trying to get away with anything that was against the rules and regulations. As the general counsel and head of compliance, I was always comfortable working with those types of people.

Then one of the non-U.S. affiliates went to Theo Duane, who was the CEO of our firm at the time, and wanted to put a group of traders in our offices to be employees of ours. I think he felt pressured to be a good corporate citizen, and so he said yes.

With all new traders or sales staff, my compliance guy and I would meet them and personally want to know who they were, what firm they came from, and what type of business they were going to conduct at our firm. I did this to understand how the firm was going to abide by the legal and compliance regulations. Financial markets are tricky, the regulations are complex, and the consequences of not being in compliance are severe, with the risk of millions of dollars in fines and potentially criminal sanctions like jail time.

After meeting with the head of the new trading group, I did not like their business one bit. Two of the guys spoke both English and Russian, and I had no issue with that. But their business was totally unrelated to what our firm did, and I thought that it was a high regulatory risk. I didn't like the types of deals that they were arranging. And the trades were not totally transparent to me or anyone else at our firm because some of the them were done in the U.S. through our firm, but they were booked on the systems of the affiliate, so we couldn't have full access to them.

Unfortunately, I hadn't been given the opportunity to say no to this group before they came. Since I had previously hired Frank Lexington, my compliance guy, my plan was to have him swing past their trading desks multiple times a day to find out what they were up to and report back to me. This went on for weeks.

It got to a point where Frank would swing by and then they would stop talking. I thought that was a bunch of crap and they weren't going to play that one on me. I decided that Frank would be stationed at their trading desk, sitting right next to them and watching everything that they did.

I thought this was very clever on my part. Then they upped it right back at me. Every day when Frank was sitting at the desk with them, they would speak only in Russian. Frank had no idea what they were saying, so they actually got one over on me, or so they thought. I pulled Frank off the trading desk and let him go back to working in his office since it was a waste of his time. I let them think that they had won, and then they went back to speaking in English.

Well nobody fucks with a Flaherty. I learned that from my dad.

Years back when I was fifteen and could only get a job working at Dunkin' Donuts for $1.65 an hour, I got fired for standing up to the boss for a girl that he was picking on for no good reason. When I got home, I was crying and my father was furious. He and my brother drove to the Dunkin' Donuts to have a word with my former boss. The owner got scared and called the police, and when they arrived, they made my family go home. When they returned, Dad was still angry. He kept saying something about taking care of it at a later time.

I am pretty sure he and another Commonwealth Edison buddy cut the power on a Friday night so they couldn't be open on their busiest day, which was Saturday. I heard him mumbling something about it and saying nobody fucks with a Flaherty. He taught me revenge is sometimes necessary and best served cold. My brother and I still laugh about Dunkin' Donuts and my dad cutting their power.

When the Russian-speaking traders thought they'd kept me in the dark, I quietly went to the senior management of our firm.

"Look, we don't know what they are up to and they know they are getting away with it. This firm has such a good reputation that it should not be risked for those guys," I said to Theo.

"You're right. We will have to get the board's approval, but we should work on that," he said.

The board agreed with me. Their business was shut down and the Russian-speaking traders left the firm.

Ha.

CHAPTER EIGHTEEN
THE REGULATORS
ARE HERE

After being at Lange and Anderson for about three years, I got an urgent call from Judy asking me to race to the reception area. I had come to learn that being summoned to the reception area meant that I was going to encounter something tricky that was already in motion. And there was no playbook or anything that prepared me for these fire drills. I hurried to the reception area, but I was tired of running.

Judy said to the group of people waiting there, "This is our general counsel."

They looked like a wolf pack of regulators. They had shown up out of the blue, which was unusual. Typically, if regulators are going to do a routine review of a firm, they provided at least one week's notice, but that didn't happen here.

"We're from the Securities Commission in Washington, DC," they said after introducing themselves.

"Welcome to Lange and Anderson." Although I tried to sound sincere, I certainly didn't mean it. In the securities industry, these people are very scary and is the group that you always want to steer clear of.

I brought them to a conference room, not the fishbowl.

"We're here to conduct an unannounced, on-site examination starting immediately. We're going to need to have working space on the premises."

This all seemed unusual to me since I was not aware of the firm doing anything wrong. Maybe there was a problem, but I reserved any judgment; I would have to see this thing through and figure it out along the way. It wasn't that some of the firms where I had worked didn't get into some trouble, but when that happened, it was typically someone making a mistake or doing something stupid but not intentional.

Working with Holly, who was our CFO, and the technology people, we were able to find desks for our new friends from the Securities Commission.

I asked, "Does your group want to see the firm's offices and trading floor?"

They did and seemed to appreciate my candor and openness. I showed them the trading floor and the different departments and introduced them to the executives at the firm.

They immediately began to ask for a lot of documents. We were very cooperative because I thought if we were not, they would think we were trying to hide something and then it could all go in a bad direction. It was very tense around the offices since we told everyone that the regulators were there and we didn't know why. People seemed to be on pins and needles knowing there was an on-site examination with no prior notice. It wasn't that anyone was afraid of them finding any bad actors, but the whole situation seemed unusual to everyone.

Holly and I were also nervous and worked late to get them everything they had asked for. When they left that day, Holly and I tried to figure out what in the heck they could be looking for. And this was the Securities Commission, so this was a big deal and very stressful, but I couldn't let on to them that I was concerned.

They came back the next day. There were many more documents that we had to provide, and we always rushed to be cooperative. I thought if we helped by quickly giving them what they needed, they might leave sooner. They came back the next day and the next.

On Monday, during the second week of this process, the lead examiner said, "Can I meet with you?"

I brought him into my office and he said, "We're wrapping it up and we will be done before the end of the day."

"Did you find anything that should be of concern to me as the general counsel?" I asked.

A credit to his honesty, he said, "No."

I sighed with relief and said, "We're trying to run a compliant organization. It is important to me. Can you share why the Securities Commission targeted our firm?"

"Oh, you were not targeted. The other Securities Commission teams have gone into other affiliated entities of banks from France on the same day. We are looking for illegal loans between affiliated entities."

It was like a sting operation that could have resulted in millions of dollars in fines for firms if they got caught in that activity.

I was right. These people were scary.

CHAPTER NINETEEN
THE WALL STREET JOURNAL

One day there was even a bigger drama, and this one was definitely over my head. The head trader of the firm, Erik Madison, called and said, "Please come to the trading floor by my desk."

It sounded serious. I wasted no time and as soon as I walked in, he said, "I got a call from the chief executive officer from Sweden Bank and he said that they had turned themselves in to the Securities Commission and the federal banking regulators."

"I was completely shocked. "What? Why?" I asked.

"We are on the other side of a two billion dollar position in ten-year U.S. Treasury securities with them. They turned themselves in and us too," he said.

I could not believe what I was hearing. How could this be happening? There had to be some mistake. That size of trade was not unusual for Lange and Anderson, but my head was spinning.

By the time I got back to my desk, the chief legal officer for Sweden Bank called to confirm that they had turned themselves and my firm over to the regulators. I had to know what on earth was going on.

"Management here doesn't fully understand the position, and they think it may be illegal," he said.

"Let me get this straight. You don't understand the trading position and you called the regulators instead of figuring it out first?" I asked.

He said, "There are some conversations on recorded lines that caused us to question the trade."

I was stunned, and he wasn't giving me much information. This entire situation still seemed like overkill, so I kept asking, "Why?"

What a colossal waste of time that was. I wanted to tell him that he was a fucking idiot, but because I wasn't sure where this issue was going, I settled for saying it out loud to myself once I had hung up the phone.

They were morons. Their first focus should have been to understand and investigate the trade or trades internally and then go to the regulators if there was a problem. To me, they did it all backward. What fucking idiots. I couldn't stop thinking that, but I had to focus on the matter at hand and related my conversation to Erik.

The next day it got worse. First thing in the morning, there was an article in the right-hand column on the front page of the *Wall Street Journal*. I always felt sorry for those who made it to that column. The people and companies in that column were usually in some sort of trouble, or at least the articles said that they were.

And there we were, the article claimed that there was an investigation by the Securities Commission and other federal regulators and it featured Lange and Anderson as the target. What I didn't know was when an article like this shows up in the *Journal*, the other news reporters from other papers try to write follow-up stories by getting some little extra piece of information. It doesn't even matter if the story is true. Some reporters can be vultures.

As soon as I saw the article, one of the administrative assistants on the trading floor, Jennifer Slope, called me.

"Hey, there is a reporter on the phone, and he wants to talk to you."

"Please tell him I'm busy."

I had no training on how to deal with reporters and something this big, but I had to act fast. I sent an email to all of the employees in the offices—including London, Paris, and Hong Kong. I told them that this story was in the *Journal* and that reporters might try to reach others at the firm. I said that any and all questions from reporters had to be referred to me and that nobody else should talk to them. Everyone was fine with that, since these kinds of inquiries can be scary.

I got a call from Mathieu Lafayette, the general counsel of the affiliated entity in New York.

"We're going to hire a spokesperson for your firm and we're going to strongly deny what is in the *Journal*," he said.

"There is no way. You can't do that. It will make the regulators angrier and then things could get worse," I said.

What an idiot.

There was too much at stake for the firm and the traders involved. Careers were potentially in jeopardy if the matter was not properly handled, and I had to do everything possible to work through this.

I decided to go over Mathieu's head. I knew that this could be very risky for me and that he could get me fired. I didn't like that guy anyway. I called Paris and spoke with Gerard at the parent bank and explained the situation. He had read the article and we had discussed the matter.

"Gerard, we can't comment to the press or this could get worse with the regulators. There's too much to risk," I said.

He kept calm and replied, "I'll take care of it."

He explained to management in Paris that he believed I was right. In the end, they all backed me, and Mathieu was told to stay out of it. I knew that he was furious, but I didn't care.

Then everything got very complicated when my administrative assistant quit after I had to tell her that her perfume was too strong and was giving everyone a headache. She said that it must be me, since nobody else had said anything to her.

I said nicely, "Because they elected me to tell you."

Also at this time, my sister-in-law was pregnant with what was going to be my first nephew. She could deliver at any minute, and I was expecting the call, but had nobody to answer my phone to screen the reporters. What a plan—that all reporter calls had to be directed to me to be screened so they could never get through and there wasn't anyone to screen them. And the phone system didn't show the caller name or phone number.

I knew that the reporters would be calling, looking for some stupid story. If I answered and said that our firm had no comment, they would likely twist it around and say that the firm had refused to comment, and they would use my name. I was concerned about saying anything, but I had to answer my phone.

Later that day, the first call came and I just picked up the phone.

"Good afternoon, Eileen Flaherty's office, may I help you?" I asked.

The person on the other end hesitated, confused. "Eileen is that you? It sounds like you."

I realized then it was Gerri, one of my industry friends. "Oh yes, sorry. I'm undercover." Which was something I never thought I would need to say to a friend over the phone. It was hilarious.

I told her all about the article in the *Journal*, about the bloodthirsty reporters who were trying to hunt me down and all the while I was waiting for an important family call.

"Only you could think to do this." She laughed.

It was hysterical.

Then more calls came. I became more confident and sounded like a good administrative assistant. And the sleazy reporters rarely identified themselves. I would answer with the same, "Good afternoon, Eileen Flaherty's office, may I help you?"

My mystery callers would then say something like, "May I speak with her?"

I would answer, "She is on a call right now."

They always asked how long the call would take and my answer was always, "It's hard to tell."

I never misrepresented anything. It was my office and I was on the phone and I didn't know how long it would take to get them to hang up. Imagine that. I beat out all of those fancy reporters from the big news organizations.

I was extra cautious, and maybe even a little paranoid, never having been through something like this before. I didn't know if the reporters knew what I looked like, but I did a fair amount of speaking on panels at industry conferences, so it was easy to look me up.

For the next few weeks, I got to the office early as always, wearing sweatpants, a baseball cap, and sunglasses. I left in the evenings, way late, after everyone else had gone, and wore the same outfit home. If they were looking to ambush me for an interview, I wasn't going to let them.

To my surprise, my efforts worked. After several weeks there were no more calls, no more articles, and let's just say that nobody ever heard any more about that article again, or the substance of what was in it. There was never a problem with the trade that caused all of this commotion to begin with. It was just the stupid Sweden Bank turning us in. To this day, I still think they are fucking idiots.

CHAPTER TWENTY

MOVING AGAIN

Very soon after ditching the reporters, my sister-in-law, Shari, had my beautiful first nephew, Ryan. That was the day that I decided that New York was wearing on me, but I had to stick it out a little longer. While working and living on the Upper West Side, I still didn't like taking the subway to work. It was better than on the east side because it was brighter, but it was too crowded, and people shoved you all the time; it was all about survival, and for me it was unpleasant.

And then there were such characters like the fish lady. There were so many days when I was on the subway going downtown to work in the morning. She would get on the train at one of the stops and then after several more stops, she would exit in Chinatown. She carried with her a huge dead fish wrapped in newspaper. The thing smelled so bad that everyone on the train was sick and gagging when the doors closed behind her. I couldn't take it anymore.

I decided to look for a new apartment. My friends Joanne and Andy Hudson had told me that I should move to Battery Park in Lower Manhattan, which was where they lived. Joanne said that it wouldn't feel like New York there, and that maybe I would like it better. My other friend David Wall said that Brooklyn Heights, which was where he lived, was a must.

One day, when I was viewing an apartment for rent, in what I thought was Brooklyn Heights, my cell phone rang, and it was David.

He asked me, "What are you doing?"

"I took your good advice and am looking for an apartment in Brooklyn Heights."

"What's the address" He seemed concerned so I read the address from the piece of paper that I had and he immediately interrupted me. "Get out of there immediately in the first cab you can. You are not in Brooklyn Heights you are across from the rough prison and you could be in danger."

He seemed to think that I could be in danger. I took his advice and high-tailed it out of there. I later learned that gang members were often visiting the prison to see their friends and trouble could break out any time.

God, this New York thing is getting ridiculous.

I was doing a lot of travel, mostly to London, and didn't have much time to look for apartments. The day before one of my trips, a realtor called me and described an apartment that was actually in Brooklyn Heights. It was a one-bedroom and it wasn't that expensive. I told him that I would meet him there within the hour.

I had to take the subway from the office, but it was only one stop. I was in a rush and spent too little time there that I didn't notice that the hallways were dark and that nobody was around. I didn't know that they didn't have a laundry room in the building.

"I'll take it, and here is the first month's rent," I said, shoving a check into his hand. Once again, I signed a two-year lease. Of course, I had to negotiate out of my two-year lease on the Upper West Side. Luckily, there were a lot of people looking for apartments in New York at the time so it didn't cost me a lot.

When I returned from London, I decided to keep some minimal furniture in New York and move the rest back to my condo in Chicago. There was a local moving company in the neighborhood, so I hired them to move the rest of my stuff to the new apartment.

It was moving day on a weekend, and the long-distance movers were done loading my stuff to go back to Chicago. The local movers were there too. They drove my stuff to my new apartment in Brooklyn Heights. They were nice guys and let me go with them in the truck.

When we arrived, we walked around the apartment, and one of the movers snorted.

"You aren't going to be here for long."

I wasn't sure what they meant and instead focused on unpacking. They helped me move my stuff inside and then I was there by myself. It was awful.

The hallways were creepy, and I didn't know anyone and didn't want to know anyone in that building. I didn't feel safe, and the movers were right—it was definitely a step down from my apartment on the Upper West Side.

I hadn't noticed before that there was a door in the kitchen that led to stairs outside. It was locked, but I thought someone could easily break in. Being afraid every night, I piled cans by the door to at least hear them in case anyone tried to break in, and I kept a kitchen knife by my bed.

And I soon realized that Brooklyn Heights was boring for to me. The main street, Montague, is a few blocks long, and that was pretty much the focus in the area or at least that is all that I found. Walking up and down Montague Street got old quickly. I noticed that mostly families that lived in Brooklyn Heights. That made sense, since it was more of a neighborhood away from crazy Manhattan, and quieter. But I was single, and although not looking to date anyone being too busy with work, I needed more of a city place again.

Within one month, I called to cancel the lease. I was getting good at negotiating my way out of two-year leases. The landlords didn't seem to mind as they could always charge the next person more.

Finally, I looked at an apartment in Battery Park, and Joanne and Andy were right all along. I should have moved there in the first place. The building was right on the water in Lower Manhattan, and there was a bike path. And best of all, it was four blocks from the office, so no more subway.

Once again, too quickly, I said, "Yes, I'll take it."

They only had one studio apartment left, which was fine since I didn't have much stuff left in New York. It had a view of the twin towers of the World Trade Center, which was nice. What I didn't notice on my whirl through to look at the apartment was that it was right next to the garbage chute room.

Once again, I went to the yellow pages to find a local mover. The last ones would have laughed at me, knowing that they were right about this place in Brooklyn Heights that I was moving out of. I called a different moving company, and they said they could do it and told me how much it would cost, so I booked them. I should have called the other guys and taken the ribbing.

On the day of the move from Brooklyn Heights to Battery Park, the movers showed up and gave me the contract to sign. I had boxed up most of my stuff and helped them move it to the truck and they drove off. I took a taxi and met them at the apartment in Battery Park.

There were two of them, and I didn't like these guys at all; it felt off. When they got to my new apartment, they started to bring in the boxes and I was unpacking. I was getting better and better at moving and could have done this as a side job on the weekends—The General Counsel of Moving.

I kept my apartment door open during the move, since my instincts were on high alert. And then it happened. They both stopped and one of them took the contract and ripped it up right in front of me. They had moved in half of my stuff.

The bigger guy said, "Unless you agree to a pay more, we're going to leave with the rest of your boxes in the truck and you will never see them again."

I stared at them, momentarily stunned. I was by myself and didn't know anyone in this building. Joanne and Andy were in a different building. I didn't know what to do.

Right then and there, I had enough of New York and lost it. I didn't care what they did to me and I wasn't going to put up with any more of this crap. In hindsight, I would never recommend for anyone to do what I did, but nobody fucks with a Flaherty.

"I'm a lawyer and calling the police on you assholes because you're criminals and committing fraud," I screamed as loud as I could.

I kept saying it and shaking while I did. I probably looked like a crazy person, but I was hoping that someone would hear me and come to help. Finally, I realized this is New York and, of course, nobody was coming to help me. My plan worked, though, and I scared the extortionist movers enough for them to backpedal.

"Okay, okay, lady, we'll finish the job."

Fucking right you'll finish the job.

I followed them to the truck, another stupid thing to do, to make sure they weren't going to drive away with the rest of my boxes. They didn't because I was standing there, and luckily there were other people around by then.

They finished the move and I paid them and, I couldn't believe it, they expected a tip from me. I am a generous tipper for service providers, but they were extortionists. I told them their tip was that I didn't call the police and suggested that they leave as fast as they could before I changed my mind. What I did was risky, but I was proud of holding my ground and not being pushed around anymore.

Oh god, maybe I am becoming a New Yorker.

After about two days into the new lease on my apartment, I noticed that there was a smell in the hallway. I was too tired to figure it out during the week and had to investigate over the weekend. It didn't take long to find out what the problem was. There was a garbage chute room right next to my new apartment. And naturally, because I was now aware of it, it became more obvious. I called and kept calling the management company to get it resolved.

Every night, I sprayed perfume in the hallway and the chute room, but the vile odors kept coming back. I was so tired and I absolutely did NOT want to move again. As efficient as I had become at moving, it was still a lot of work. I lost my patience and called the management office again.

"Look, I don't want to keep calling you and you don't want to keep hearing from me. I need another apartment away from the garbage chute now."

The gal who ran the office said, "We have one coming available in a month, and it'd be in the other building across the driveway area."

"I'll take it," I said and couldn't wait to get out of there.

I saw the new apartment and it wasn't near the garbage chute. It was another studio, and it was in the building where Joanne and Andy lived. It was a much nicer building. My view was of the building across the courtyard, but I also had a sliver of a view of the Statue of Liberty. This was going to be so much better.

I needed help with the move, but I certainly wasn't going to use the extortionist movers again, and the other local company with the nice guys would know how many times I had moved. Since it was a move to another building in the same complex, I thought that maybe a maintenance guy and a buddy of his would be interested in helping me for some extra cash on the side. I approached one of the guys who seemed nice and he jumped at the chance. I had to be out that Saturday, so we agreed on a time.

That morning, I started to move my clothes to the new building. It was a lot of trips, as my wardrobe had grown substantially. Since New York was wearing on me, I thought I deserved something new every weekend. After moving all of the clothes for hours, the maintenance guy still wasn't there. I didn't have his number, as he said he would be there and he seemed reliable.

I had no choice but to move everything else by myself. I got to a point of being so sore that I could barely move. Finally, I started using a shopping cart that was in the lobby. I thought, "I am the general counsel of a Wall Street firm, and I am moving to a new apartment in a shopping cart."

I knew that if I called Joanne and Andy, they would have helped me, but I didn't want to bother them.

Luckily, after some time, I noticed that there was another move that day and they had a real moving company. After moving everything that I could, except for the larger items like my bed, a glass table, and a few other things, I approached the real movers and explained my situation.

"When you're done with your move, would you please help me? I am exhausted and the guy who was supposed to help me didn't show up."

They were nice guys and they said, "Sure, we'll help."

At least they didn't seem like criminals, and honestly, I was almost too tired to care. They helped me and it was finished. It took me eight hours to move that day. I collapsed in bed that night and it took days to recover.

I liked the new apartment much better. The building seemed cleaner and brighter. Joanne and Andy came to see my place and insisted that I borrow their card table and a chair so that I would at least have a place to sit and eat. It wasn't that I was cheap or anything; I wasn't planning on staying long. They thought it was funny that the only things in my refrigerator were wine and chocolate. What else did I need?

I soon decided that this was my last move in New York and then there would be one final move—one that would be back to Chicago. I was missing my nephew Ryan, and he was too important in my life. I was not going to be some long-distance aunt who shows up at Christmas with gifts. I didn't want to miss out on his life.

I think that was the best personal decision I have ever made, that my family was always going to come first. And my second beautiful nephew, Dan, came two years later. I was actually there right after he was born, and my finger was the first one that he grabbed. I was so busy with my career that I never got married or had kids, but Ryan and Dan were so important to me.

No job was ever bigger to me than that. I had to figure out how to get back to Chicago for good.

CHAPTER TWENTY-ONE
GOING HOME

On one of my flights from Chicago back to New York, I decided to come up with a plan to get back home. Lange and Anderson had a small Chicago office, and why couldn't I work out of there one week a month? That way I would have the whole week after work and two weekends to spend with Ryan, and then later Dan. It seemed to me like a good and reasonable compromise. I had seen so many people in my career who missed school events, games, and regular hanging-out time because their jobs came first. That was not going to be me.

When I got back to New York, I waited until the middle of the week to carry out my plan. I didn't want to do it the first two days back, as it would have looked too obvious. I was going to ask Joe, the CEO, if I could work out of the firm's Chicago office one week a month, and that it wouldn't cost the firm any money since I would pay for the airfare and had my condo in Chicago. It would cost me plenty, but it would be worth it.

By midweek, Joe seemed like he was in an okay mood, which was not always the case, so I walked up to him on the trading desk and said, "Do you have a few minutes?"

I laid it out how working from Chicago made sense and wouldn't cost the firm any money. "It might be better for the firm because I could get more done in Chicago, with fewer distractions."

I thought that my presentation was perfect and compelling. Without even thinking about it, he flat out said, "No. Your presence in the New York office is too important."

While it was flattering that he thought that much of me, I couldn't leave it at that.

"Would you think about it some more?" I asked too quickly.

"No."

I probably should have waited a bit to do that, but I was anxious to get home. I was blown away that my plan had failed. I thought about it that evening and decided that I had one more shot, but it was very risky. I decided that if it didn't work, I would stay long enough to get my next bonus and then quit. Family was coming first.

My final plan was to go to the chairman of the company, Charlie Bond, and lay it out for him. I explained to him its efficiency and that it wouldn't cost the firm any money.

"That would be fine," he said.

Now the hard part was going back to Joe and telling him what I had done to get what I wanted. As I've mentioned before, I always got the sense that he didn't like me, so I figured there wasn't much I could to do make him like me less. He was on the trading desk and I approached him.

"Charlie said that the Chicago thing would be okay with him."

I could tell that he was furious. His face was getting red. He didn't say anything but got up and walked away. He wasn't happy with me and that was unfortunate, but it was worth it.

The split-time arrangement started out as one week a month in Chicago, and it went very smoothly. I kept up my end of the bargain, being productive and always knocking out the work. Then Charlie left, and I worried that this arrangement was going to get reversed. It didn't, and the whole thing worked out.

Then a new CEO, Josh Garden, came in and I worried all over again. He had also become the new chairman, so each new guy could potentially put my whole situation at risk. It ended up that Josh was fine with my Chicago gig and thought I could even spend more time there. He was happy with my work, and how I made the arrangement go smoothly for everyone. I liked Josh and thought he did a good job.

Eventually, I spent two weeks a month in Chicago and then three. One day, I decided to float the idea of being based in Chicago and coming to New York as needed. To my shock, Josh was fine with it. Yeah, I was going to have one last final move and it was back to Chicago. My plan worked. I had had enough of those New York moves, and that city was not for me.

Not long after moving back to Chicago, I realized that going to New York and all that hell for almost two years was one of the best career moves I had ever made. I got to keep my New York–level salary and bonus and live back in Chicago. New York money goes a long way in good old Chicago.

I decided to leave most of my things in New York, so I didn't need movers this time. I didn't want the memories and I boxed up my clothes and the few items that I was keeping. I gave the folding table and chair back to Joanne and Andy and left the bed and the rest of my stuff. It was all in good condition, so maybe the people who worked in the building or someone else could use it. Goodbye, New York.

CHAPTER TWENTY-TWO

MERGER MANIA

Since Lange and Anderson wasn't making money and the fung shway thing didn't work out, there was what is known on Wall Street as downsizing. It means that a bunch of people get fired for no reason except that the firm needs to cut costs. I hated the downsizing part and, as the general counsel, I had to be involved in the legal documentation.

The firm was generous with severance, which was not typical on Wall Street, but it still meant that those nice people would have uncertainty until they could get another job. Many of them had been at the firm for a long time, and some of them for their whole careers. It was awful. I did everything to try to help the people affected by giving recommendations, calling other firms to see if they were hiring people, and trying to be as decent as I could to each person.

Then one day, without any warning, there was an article in the *Wall Street Journal* that three banks in France would merge to become one entity, and that all of their affiliated entities around the world within the organizations would be merged. One of those banks owned my firm.

Oh my god, this was going to be one huge deal.

It was going to be a global monster merger.

We were all shocked at the firm, especially because it was kept such a secret that we had to read about it in the newspaper. And, from what I knew, mergers weren't really mergers. Although entities could combine and form one legal entity, in practice they didn't merge. There were the winners and losers. If you were on the strong badge, employed by the stronger company, then life was good. If you were on the badge of the company that effectively got taken over, you didn't want to stay since you would become yesterday's trash waiting at the curb to be picked up by the garbage truck.

The three banks didn't waste much time. Within about a month, they had a plan of how it was going to work and gave us a proposed timeline. They must have been planning this for some time to have had all of this figured out, which made it even more surprising that it wasn't leaked before we read about it in the news.

Oddly enough, about a month before the announcement, I thought that the shares of the parent bank of my company were undervalued in the market, so I bought some. I was willing to make that bet, and we were not prohibited from those trades at the time.

After the merger announcement, the shares of the parent bank of my company tripled in value. I made a good amount of money but was then afraid to sell the shares. I knew that the regulators could pick up in their surveillance systems when the shares of a company rise in a short time frame, and who has held the shares for a short period of time and then sells them to make a big profit.

They can then bring a criminal case for insider trading. I didn't have any inside information but decided to wait a year to sell the shares, to be on the safe side. After a year, the shares of the combined company were worth far less than the price that I paid for them. This was my worst trade of all time. So much for a successful merger.

When the executives of the parent bank of my firm came to us with the plan, they told us that there were going to be three entities in the U.S., with affiliated companies in London, Paris, and Hong Kong merging together. I was certain that it was going to be a mess. It was also interesting that they were going to let the companies do the merger themselves. They didn't have an outside group doing the whole thing, which is how most other large mergers work.

I went to talk to Olivier Honore, our French liaison.

"I can do all of the legal and regulatory work for the merger of our company, as well as the other entities in the U.S and their non-U.S. affiliates," I said. The parent banks were focused on their mergers.

"It'll easily save the organizations in the seven figures, rather than having it done by outside law firms," I said.

That piqued his interest. He knew as did I that some law firms can totally charge huge amounts in legal fees for something like this.

It was a huge risk on my part to offer to take on this project because it was going to be a massive amount of work, and I was on my own and had never done it before. Olivier and the management of my company liked the idea since it could give our company a stronger hand in the whole process, which was why I offered to do it in the first place. To my shock, the other companies agreed. At that time, they had no ax to grind with me since I wasn't a business threat, or so they thought.

Oh, this was going to be wicked fun.

Each of the entities had multiple offices and several had affiliated entities in other countries, and it was all part of the process. There were entities in the U.S., London, Paris, and Hong Kong. I was going to have to figure all of this out and wasn't even confident that it was possible, but everyone seemed to have faith in me. They respected my legal and compliance skills, and my reputation, so I couldn't let my firm down. I would work hard like my parents taught me and make it happen if I could.

Since all of the entities in scope were owned by each of the three parent banks, and the decision to merge was already made, there was no reason for any deep due diligence or confrontational negotiations. We had no choice in the matter, as it was going to happen, so I took a practical and cost-effective approach.

I got hold of the legal structures of each of the companies, created a listing of the regulators and exchanges that would have to approve this, and mapped out my plan. There were about twenty regulators and exchanges that I would have to deal with, although one of the more contentious entities wanted to deal with their primary regulator themselves. And there were hundreds of agreements and contracts that would have to be dealt with too.

In presenting my plan to the executives of the three companies, it seemed to make sense to them, so I started working on it right away. I soon realized how big this thing was, but I couldn't let anyone know that I was drowning, and I couldn't let myself fail. I took the same approach as that first day in college—to work harder than I could and to keep going even when I didn't think I could.

As time went on in the merger process, everyone at each firm hated those at the other firms, and there were no friends except your own colleagues. Nobody outside of your own organization could be trusted.

Everyone had the same goal, which was to be the lead surviving firm and save all the jobs of your own people. We were told that the merger date had to be specifically September 30, 2001. The three parent banks were to be combined on that day, so all of this across the globe had to happen on the same day.

Nobody knew then what would transpire between then and the end of September 2001.

When the merger months were playing out, it became clear that Josh, whom I liked and was our CEO, was not going to get the lead CEO position of the combined entities. That was too bad since I truly thought that he was the most qualified. But mergers are all about politics, and it was going to go to the guy at one of the other firms, whom I didn't like at all.

Tom, whom I liked too and was our COO, was going to be the lead running a division in the combined entity, and the guys from the other firms weren't going to get that job. He had won so far. I was glad since Tom was a good guy, and we still laugh about all the dirty merger tricks to this day. That is the way mergers work—you try to get the upper hand and hold on to it for dear life.

Some of the tricks of one of the other companies were plain criminal. There was the illegal tapping of the phones in the conference room where our executives met with theirs and had to make calls expecting privacy. There was an ethical employee of that company who called and told us about the tapping and that she was not comfortable with their actions. We appreciated her honesty and didn't use any phones anymore when we visited their offices.

But we had our share of tricks too—like in Hong Kong, which I will describe soon—but not nearly sinister like theirs. The CEO of one of the companies that we were to merge with, Paul, said we had too many international phone lines and that we should cut costs. They picked which ones. Our head of technology, who was a smart gal, Debra Central, came into my office.

"They picked our main transatlantic phone line to cut. If we do that, then on the day of the merger, there will be no connection to the combined offices in Europe and Asia. Nobody in the firm's offices outside of the U.S. will be able to conduct any business. What should we do?" she asked.

I smiled and said, "Don't worry, I will take care of it."

I called that asshole, Paul, who was going to have a senior role in the combined companies.

"Hey, Paul, are you sure you want us to cut all of these lines?" I asked.

I didn't highlight which lines in particular. He was a smart guy, right?

"Yes."

"Are you sure?" I asked. Oh, this was going to be rich.

"We know what we're doing," he said smugly.

"Okay."

I smiled and hung up and then relayed what he had said back to Debra.

"Don't stop them. They know what they're doing, according to Paul," I told her.

We laughed. We had tried to help them.

Sadly, Paul's crew finally figured out what it meant to cut that main transatlantic line and halted the order to cut the connection just in time. Damn.

Since it was clear that Josh was not going to be the lead of the whole combined company, he wanted to leave, and it was all worked out for him to depart professionally. That was the first in a number of tough steps. He was a classy guy and had been through mergers before, which meant he understood this stuff far better than I did.

The spy guy, Thierry Boucher—the guy from another firm who got stationed at our firm and occupied the jinxed office during the merger—was a total asshole. It was clear that he was bright, but he was not going to be our friend. Initially, I liked him, then I realized that that was a waste of my time. He made it clear that he was a political animal and there to support his bank, not the people in my firm.

Everything was going to be done behind people's backs. The people at my firm all realized this and we decided that we could play that game too. It became a daily sport. If that was the way this whole thing would be played out, we had to step up our game and be better at it than they were.

The other companies in the combined merger didn't have general counsels at the time, so my parent bank wanted me to get that job for the combined U.S. companies and the non-U.S. affiliates. I don't know if behind the scenes the other companies fought or supported my move into that position, but I suspect that no one outside of my company was too thrilled.

The merger work continued and occupied most of my time. It was interesting; I learned a lot and was delivering. There were plenty of people waiting for me to make a misstep, and I wouldn't let that happen. I worked seven days a week but pretended that I was working regular hours, and that was no big deal. I knew that if I showed any sign of weakness, they would pounce. And, of course, all the executives at the other companies were men.

I was constantly flying to London, Paris, and Hong Kong. It was all part of the process of getting this merger thing done. I was totally exhausted and living on caffeine while the knife fights and backstabbing continued around me, growing nastier and nastier.

There were such dirty tricks, most of which I can't talk about not knowing if the statute of limitations has passed. We didn't start them, but we jumped right in and made sure that no one one-upped us. Soon it became the norm to engage in more tricks that were less obvious, so we always had plausible deniability. With Thierry in the jinxed office, our offices now felt more like an occupied territory.

I couldn't stand him, and the feeling appeared to be mutual. He looked like he had black eyes. Thierry looked demonic to me. I did as much as possible to intentionally annoy him. It started to be more and more clear to Tom, our then CEO, who was to be the head of the combined derivatives business, that they were not being straight with us.

In these situations, it can be very stressful, and while some people might crumple under the strain, my approach was "bring it on." Fortune favors the bold. We were going to fight for every employee of our company.

There were many merger meetings, and I was a feature at each as the regulatory, exchange, and clearing house approvals were crucial to get before September 30, 2001, the merger date. If they didn't come in time, then the merger couldn't take place, and that would be a big problem for each of the banks involved.

There was another all-day merger meeting scheduled for the executives of the companies, and it was such a waste of time since I had real work to do.

Nobody else was doing anything to make the merger happen, and I had no time to sit there for an entire day.

The room was filled with the guys from each of the firms all happy to sit there all day and do nothing. I was the only woman in the room for these meetings, except for the gals who had to get coffee for those suited-up assholes from the other firms.

Before the meeting, I had asked a colleague, Richard Harlem, to call me on my cell phone thirty minutes after the start time. Thirty minutes went by and there was no call. Another few minutes went by, then the call came. I answered it and faked a look like there was a new and terrible disaster happening somewhere. Everyone stopped since I was supposed to be their entertainment for the meeting. I stood up and put my hand over the phone.

"I have an important call. I'll be back as soon as possible," I said, making sure the whole room could hear me. I gathered my piles of documents and raced out the door. I didn't lie, it was an important call to me to get me out of that room.

I am sure they thought that it was some important regulator that I was speaking to, and what could be more important? I immediately went to see Richard.

"What took you so long?"

We both laughed, as he knew exactly what was going on.

I didn't make it back to the meeting because I didn't want to.

I used that technique several times through my career and it always worked. Each time, another group fell for it. Once, there was an all-day seminar in the beautiful French countryside, and I got put on the group to discuss bank capital charges all afternoon in a stuffy conference room. I once again had someone call me thirty minutes in and said there was an important client and that I was in the middle of a negotiation that could cost the firm a lot of money if it didn't go well. I said I would be back as quickly as I could, and they all understood. I went back to my room and sipped champagne and took a nap. Another success with that trick.

Working hard on the merger, I had to see our resident spy guy, Thierry, all the time. And although I was professional, neither one of us tried very hard to disguise that we couldn't stand each other. I had previously described our nice offices and what we called the "hall of fame." That was where the formal portraits of all of the former chairmen of Lange and Anderson were located. It was very impressive.

One day, Tom walked into my office with a camera.

"Pose for a picture like you're going to yell, 'You'd better not do that.'"

I was good at saying that when I needed to. He snapped the photo and, ever curious, I asked, "What're you up to?"

"You'll see," he said with a wicked smile.

A few days later, one of the portraits of a former chairman in the hall of fame had been replaced with the picture of me blown up and put in the fancy frame. And it was hung right on the wall outside of Thierry's jinxed office. Every time he went in or out of his office, he had to walk past me. He had no way to avoid my picture. It was hysterical, and there was nothing that he could do. These were our offices he was occupying, and this was the property of our firm. It wasn't his yet, and we made sure he knew it.

Right after the merger, my portrait mysteriously disappeared, and I am pretty sure that someone still has it in his basement. He wasn't going to let Thierry and his crew burn it or throw it out the first chance they got. Tom and I still laugh about this one whenever we catch up.

CHAPTER TWENTY-THREE

A SAD DAY

It was the beginning of September 2001, and the merger was on track to take place at the end of the month. The exchange, clearing house, and regulatory approvals that I was working on were coming in and on time. Hundreds of agreements were ready to be transferred, and the Herculean efforts were paying off. I was exhausted and couldn't wait for it to be over. And then it happened.

This is not a story about 9/11, and it's not my place to write one. But the timing did impact the merger, so I mention the effects and how it changed the course of what was to happen.

I was working in Chicago that week and had a flight scheduled to go to New York on the morning of 9/11. I was working on many time-sensitive parts of the merger, and the travel would have slowed me down, so I postponed the flight for a day.

On my way to the Chicago office that morning, the first terrorist attack happened. When I got to the Chicago office, we didn't know what to do. We were petrified for our colleagues in the New York office and couldn't reach them by phone. Our New York office was a few blocks away from the World Trade Center, and we didn't know if everyone was okay.

Our offices in Chicago were adjacent to the Sears Tower, and there were rumors that it was also a target that morning for a terrorist attack.

"We're all immediately leaving the building. I think this is a terrorist attack on New York and nobody knows where else it will hit," I said to everyone in the office.

I couldn't get through to anyone in the New York office. I tried nonstop for the next twenty-four hours, frantic and worried, until finally Holly answered her cell phone.

"Everyone who was in the office is okay. It was bad but we're all okay," she said.

"Thank god."

Within about three weeks, the people who worked in my firm were able to access the New York office again. Prior to that, all businesses were blocked off to allow emergency personnel to do their jobs. Key people from the New York office had driven together to the Chicago office, and the firm was able to operate to process critical information.

It was a horrible time in the U.S. and all over the world because nobody could believe that could have ever happen. Despite all this merger stuff, I was sympathetic to one of the merging firms, located in the World Financial Center, who had lost some of the directors of their affiliate company located in the World Trade Center. They had also lost a lot of their friends that day.

Given all of what was going on, the three parent banks agreed to complete their merger on time, but to postpone the merger of the U.S. entities and their non-U.S affiliates. This was going to be a huge amount of work for me, but I didn't mind at all, under the circumstances.

During this time, I was touched by the good in people who came out in droves to help, and also by how accommodating the exchanges, clearing houses, and regulators around the world were. It was as if everyone wanted to do something to help anyone or any firm in New York.

While all of this was going on, the political power of one of the entities in the merger had become stronger. Within months, it became apparent that my firm was losing, or had lost, the power position in derivatives and that Tom was no longer going to be the lead of the derivatives business. What this meant was that most of the people from my firm would lose their jobs, and if they didn't, they would be from "the other company" and most of them wouldn't be wanted.

Tom had become the CEO of our company after Josh had left, and he decided that he had had enough and no longer wanted to work with those people, so he resigned. There were only a few months left before the final merger date and there was no CEO. My parent bank wanted the company to run separately until the merger, so they elected me to be the CEO. I was the CEO, general counsel, head of compliance, anti-money laundering, and corporate secretary. And, I was doing the merger. I was scared to death with all of those titles; if something went wrong, the regulators could hold me accountable.

I had too much to do, but I had to pull it off.

The company at this point was substantially smaller, with only the derivatives business left, but it was still a lot of responsibility. But I had to keep it going and try and fight as hard as I could for our employees and their jobs.

Then the board of my company did something unique. They decided that if any employee wanted to leave, they could elect to do so on their own and still get their severance and any other payments owed and not have any restrictions that would keep them from going to any other company. That never happens on Wall Street, but the board realized that these people did nothing wrong, and that it probably would not be pleasant for them to work in the combined organization.

Not surprisingly, all employees, except for a very few, elected to leave on the day of the merger, and I was going to be right out the door with them. The people in the other companies were not our kind of people and were never going to be. I think the other company that had gained the stronger position in the merger found out about everyone leaving after we were all gone.

Oh, sorry. Forgot to tell you. Best of luck to you.

Something else happened during that merger that still brings a smile to my face. My company had an office in Hong Kong. The people who worked there were incredibly dedicated. When the merger was originally announced, I was able to get approval from the management of my company to pay retention bonuses for all of the staff there. A retention bonus is an extra amount that applies if a person stays through to a specific date, which is typically during something rocky.

When the merger got postponed due to the 9/11 tragedy, the team there was paid their retention amounts. With all the dirty tricks going on, I did my best.

I called Jeff, the CEO of one of the other merging companies that also had an office in Hong Kong. Ours and theirs were to be combined, so I couldn't make some decisions on my own. I said, "These people in our Hong Kong office are necessary to keep things running smoothly through the new merger date, so I have to pay them retention bonuses."

"No. We're not doing it, and I'm going to make sure you can't do it yourself," he said.

He thought he was going to block me. He thought he was so much smarter than me.

"Fine by me," I said and hung up on him.

Well, that's the short version of our conversation. But then I had to call the people in the Hong Kong office and explain what had happened, that I had done everything to get them paid, but it wasn't going to happen. Well, a few days later, "I heard" that they were all in the office, and after eating half of their lunches, they all left and quit.

The other company didn't know for some time, and I must have forgotten to tell them. I also heard that the regulator there was furious with the other company because they couldn't reconcile their books for months after the merger. Our people weren't there to help them. The Hong Kong offices must have stunk to high heaven with the old food sitting there, rotting for who knows how long. Now that was funny.

During the last few months, I had the big titles and basically had to effectively shut down the company. I was the last CEO of this great Wall Street boutique firm. That was sad because it had been around for more than fifty years and, even though it was not huge, it had a great reputation. What a shame to let all of that go. It didn't seem like a good business decision to me.

But those making the decisions were obviously so smart that the stock of the combined entities is now priced at a third of what I paid for it. Must be some geniuses who let those types keep their jobs.

CHAPTER TWENTY-FOUR

BOXES

It was the last few weeks before the actual merger and I had everything in order from the legal and regulatory perspective. The legal documentation, exchange, clearing house, and regulatory approvals were all done. The hundreds of contracts and agreements had been addressed too.

I was very proud of my work, especially since I hadn't done it before. At the same time as this chapter in my life was coming to an end, I was heartbroken. I was going to miss the job that I had come to love and working with the people whom I so respected. And we had achieved great things in business and were finally making money. I had to keep stopping myself from thinking about this all the time.

Nobody from the other companies said thanks for saving tons or money or for the hard work on the merger, but I didn't respect any of them, so it didn't matter to me. I had decided some time ago that my success was defined by me and not anyone else; I had gotten over that first-grade thing a long time ago.

All of the documentation for the merger was in several boxes in the Chicago office. I had complete files with backup copies there too, as some of the derivatives operations people were nice enough to help me with the copying. Of course, I kept electronic copies too.

On the day of the merger, I went through the files again to make sure they were all in good order and they were. I wasn't sure what was going to happen to all of these boxes, but after that day, it wasn't my problem to worry about. I packed a box of my personal stuff. It wasn't much—some books, pictures, and souvenirs from the industry.

Everyone left the office, and I was the last one there. I wasn't in a hurry to leave because, after that day, the firm would be gone and my job would be over. I walked around the office again one last time, in tears. So much had happened there and now it was silence.

I left the keys and my identification badge on the desk, shut the lights off, and left for the last time.

I woke up the next day and couldn't believe how tired I was. This merger had been taking its toll, but I couldn't think about that while I had all of that responsibility. A few months earlier, I had been interviewing for a new position. It was for a larger organization with its main office in New York and an office in Chicago. I was working to be based in Chicago even though it would require a lot of travel back and forth. Things weren't moving along quickly enough, so I needed to figure out something else.

We had a family event the weekend before the end of Lange and Anderson, at our house in Burbank. My parents, Kevin, Shari, Ryan, and Dan were there. Dan was little and tired and wanted some fresh air, so Kevin and I sat in their minivan with him in the driveway, which seemed to calm him down.

I said to Kevin, "I don't know what to do because the other job hasn't come through yet and maybe it won't. I need a cover so those assholes from the other companies won't know that I don't have a job yet. I don't want to give them the satisfaction."

Kevin, my wonderful brother, said, "You should form your own consulting business."

Why hadn't I thought of that before?

We were thinking of big names to make it sound important. He said it needed to have *global* in the name, so I came up with The Global Capital Group Ltd. That sounded important. That week, I filed the formation documents, and The Global Capital Group Ltd. was born. This was going to be a new and big chapter in my life. Although I was sad about Lange and Anderson and what was to happen later in the week, I had something to build from scratch, something new to focus on.

Before leaving the office on the last day in Chicago, I had one last fun thing to do. I left a message on my work voicemail that if anyone wanted to reach me, I was at The Global Capital Group Ltd. and included the phone number.

I knew that the other merged companies would eventually figure it out, I didn't know how long it would take them to do so, but I didn't care. There was nobody left that I wanted calls directed to. I knew that would make them furious when they finally found the message.

I called my voicemail for almost a month and then it was disconnected. It took them long enough. That was a good last laugh.

The Monday after the merger, I was at home and got a call from Thierry—the spy guy with the black eyes, who was now heading the combined firm. I should have let it go to voicemail but thought it might be someone that I used to work with who might need something.

"Hello?" I immediately realized it was him. There was no small talk or how-are-yous.

"Where is the merger?" His clipped tone told me all I needed about how this call was going to go.

"What are you talking about?" I asked.

"Where is the merger?" His tone was more urgent, if that was possible. I could tell he was getting angry. I liked that.

We went back and forth a few more times, then he finally shouted, "Where is the proof of the merger?"

"Oh," I paused intentionally. "It is in the boxes," I said patiently, trying to annoy him even more for how badly I thought he treated all of our employees when he was in our offices.

"What boxes?"

"Your fucking merger is in boxes on the table in the conference room in Chicago. There's your merger. The other box is mine with instructions to ship it to my condo."

You see while I was doing the merger work, I didn't send copies of anything to him or anyone else outside of our company. He didn't ask and I didn't offer. Everything was in good order, and my company had electronic copies too, but I didn't owe him or anyone else anything more.

Your fucking merger is in boxes—I so liked saying that.

He was speechless, realizing that he let this happen to himself. I hung up and laughed for a long time.

As entertaining as that was, I did find out that they had seized my box of personal belongings. That was a low blow. My antics were amusing, but what they did was not. They had no reason to seize my personal items. I called Paola, a very senior executive at the combined firm, whom I liked, and she said she would try to find out what was going on.

Paola later came back to me and said, "I'm so sorry. They are going through the box to make sure there was nothing from the merger or company property in it."

"Don't worry and thanks for looking into it," I said.

How stupid of those guys. If I had wanted to remove any property of the firm surely it wouldn't have been left behind in that box. I would have removed items months ago.

What assholes.

I never did take anything and never would have. It wouldn't be ethical. My parents had taught me better. It was more confirmation that I could never have worked with people like that anyway. They obviously looked at me and could only see themselves, and that was not how I rolled. After waiting for weeks, I finally got my box back.

Almost a month after leaving Lange and Anderson, the new job offer that I had been waiting for came. It was going to be based in Chicago and at that good old New York salary and bonus that I had been getting, so I accepted it.

CHAPTER TWENTY-FIVE

BACK IN CHICAGO

I was excited to start my new job as the associate general counsel at Scotland International Bank. I was going to have responsibility for the legal, compliance and anti-money laundering teams. I was also going to be the chief ethics officer. I liked that title.

The merger had been more stressful than I had realized at the time, and until I had the new job offer, my time off didn't feel like time off. I found that you are not really on vacation if you are between jobs with uncertainty even if only for a several weeks.

I started in the Chicago office and spent the first week there and had a decent office but nothing like the one from my last job or the really cool one at the derivatives exchange. It seemed that this firm didn't waste money on things like nice, fancy offices for the executives. Maybe that is why they were making money and the last firm hadn't figured that out. There was no fung shway guy either.

I met with my new team in Chicago and liked everyone there. There was the compliance team with six people and the anti-money laundering team with four people. Each of the members of my new team was smart and bright and wanted to work hard to maintain the good reputation of our firm. The guys and gals on the team became my friends and they still are. They were all talented, and I could also see the value that I could bring too. The work was going to be what I liked, and the people were good.

The firm did business in derivatives, which was my specialty now, and also securities, which I had learned in my last job. Scotland International Bank was pretty big and was part of a larger global organization that was owned by a parent Scottish bank. I liked the Scottish and the international aspect of it and was also hoping to get some trips to Scotland. International travel in business class paid for by someone else was one of my favorite things to do.

I finished the first week, which is always the hardest in any job. Everything was different, and I was the new animal at the zoo for all to look at. But I'd survived so many new jobs, these transitions had become normal for me.

The senior people at the firm had been there a long time, and they said they were interested in my ideas and how other firms did things differently or better. Coming from my last job, I could give them some ideas to consider, they thought. I took them seriously and after a few weeks gave them some suggestions and then some more.

I also noticed when they stopped listening; it was clear they thought I was complaining. I wasn't, but I had taken them at their word that they were interested in how other firms did things differently. I learned that when a firm says that, they don't mean it. They like everything the way it is and want nothing changed. That was fine with me. After that, I kept my ideas for improvement to myself. No sense in wasting them.

The next week, I flew to the New York offices where I had a small company office. The firm was right on Seventh Avenue near Times Square and I loved the location. I met with my legal and compliance teams there and had the same impression. There were seven compliance people and two anti-money laundering people on my New York team. Nice and talented people doing their best to represent the firm and keep people out of trouble. I was welcomed by all, and many of them became my friends too and still are.

They walked me around the trading floor and to the different departments. There were a lot of people to meet. I had a sneaking suspicion that there might be some shady trading going on because people became quiet when I was around the trading floor, but it was too early to put my finger on it. After the first day, I went back to my hotel and collapsed.

I hated almost every hotel in New York. There was a list of approved hotels, and I could only stay in those. I stayed in many and always ended up moving rooms several times. They were all awful. They were expensive, and most of them were not as clean they should have been.

Once, I was staying at a particular dump of a hotel up on Seventh Avenue. When I got back from work that evening, a dog that was barking in a room a few doors away. Loudly. And not stopping any time soon.

I called the front desk and said, "What is a dog doing in this hotel?"

"We allow service dogs in this hotel," the front desk manager said.

"Well, if it is a service dog, the owner has either left it in a room—hence, it is not a service dog—or the owner is in there, dead. Get me another room fast before all the other guests want to move rooms and you don't have any left."

The hotel reception guy got the message that I meant business and moved me to another room.

Another hotel that was on the approved list frequently had mold in the bathroom. I would often switch rooms at that hotel and was told at one point when checking in that they had my name at the front desk and they were supposed to give me any room that I wanted. It does go to show that the squeaky wheel gets the grease. I finally realized later that was one of the reasons I hated New York hotels.

The following weeks became easier as they always do in a new job. I had more people to meet and plenty of work to do. I quickly learned that some of the business people were aggressive in bringing in new clients. They would promise things that we then had to make work from a legal perspective. This seemed to be another reason why they were making money. It also made the job interesting as things were always moving at the speed of light. In spite of the fast pace, my team was very compliance minded and careful in their work.

I also learned rather quickly that if a business person there didn't like my answer, they would go around me to get to do what they wanted. That was incredibly frustrating. There was one business guy who wanted to open a particular type of securities account. I was not comfortable with it, so I said no. My firm did business only with large institutions and this would be a personal account of a friend of his. Well, of course, he didn't like my answer and went to the CEO of the firm, Bonnie Bryant, who came to me.

"Isn't there a way that you can make this work?"

"We will look at it again, but no promises. We represented to the Federal Research Bank, our regulator, that we only do business with institutional accounts and this isn't one. It's a personal account," I said. I was glad that she didn't push it and let the issue drop.

My answers were well researched. I was not a push over, and I would never give an answer that someone wants rather than the correct answer. I was not going to like these firm politics at all.

I did get to go to the London and Scotland offices several times. That was the best part, and flying business class, and they paid for all of it. And I got to keep the frequent flier miles that I earned for flying for my personal use. That was the best. Although, when I had time off, the last thing that interested me was to get anywhere near an airport.

Team building and mentoring the younger staff were what I loved the most. That was an important role to me—to help others in their careers—and wished that I had had the opportunity to work more with people like me earlier in my career.

As much as I liked many aspects of my job, it was exhausting. I would work in the Chicago office on Monday and set the alarm for four-fifteen on Tuesday morning. Monday night would be spent packing for the week. I could never sleep on those Monday nights, always afraid of sleeping through the alarm and missing the flight to New York. I would land on Tuesday morning at LaGuardia airport and have the same drill almost every week—race to get to the New York office as I had already lost time traveling and they were an hour ahead of Chicago.

I just had to make it through Tuesdays. Wednesdays were better as I could sleep on Tuesday nights because of being so tired and just collapsing. Although, living in a hotel every week was starting to suck. I went to the same Chinese restaurant on 57th Street every time I was there. The owners there were nice to me.

On Thursday morning, I would pack up, check out of the hotel, and head to the office dragging my carry-on suitcase. I would work through the day and then head to LaGuardia airport for the flight back to Chicago. I generally got in late and then had to work in the Chicago office on Friday. The weekends were spent catching up on sleep because the weeks were so brutal. I would always spend Saturdays with Ryan and Dan and made it my most important job to be alert so we could have fun. Then Sunday was spent getting ready to do this all over again.

Then one day, my personal life changed forever. I was in New York, and it was early Thursday afternoon. I had to head to LaGuardia in a few hours. I was in my office and my brother called.

He said, "Mom had a bad heart attack and you have to get here fast."

I wasted no time and ran down the hall crying and out of the building. I got into the first cab that I could and got on an earlier flight to Chicago.

The people around me on the plane knew that something was wrong, so everyone was silent. When we landed in Chicago, I went straight to Northwestern Hospital and raced to intensive care. It's too hard to write about this, but several days later, she passed away.

My dad was never prepared to lose her and we weren't either. After a few years of giving it his best, he passed away. His heart was just broken. I was sad when he died, but also glad that he didn't have to suffer any longer.

I miss them both.

After almost two years on the job and all of the traveling drudgery, I finally realized why I hated the hotels so much. I didn't want to be there. The job was going okay, but it was exhausting. I was also sick and tired of people going around me to get the answers they wanted. My answers were correct and would keep the firm and its people out of trouble. I resented anyone who tried to go behind my back.

Then there was the trip that made me realize something more important than making all of this money, which I loved.

I was at LaGuardia on a Thursday night, waiting to board the flight back to Chicago. Luckily, I ran into another gal, Gail Randolph, from the Chicago office, and we were good friends. We were supposed to be on the same flight.

The flight was delayed, so we hung around and it wasn't a big deal since flights were always delayed at LaGuardia. But I was a master traveler by this time and could read all of the signs of trouble. There was severe weather, and flights were being cancelled left and right. When your plane is delayed, always ask at the airport where your plane is regardless of the time they tell you the flight would leave. If the plane is still on the ground at the gate of another airport in another city, then the departure time they are giving you is just a made-up lie. The airlines do this all the time.

To my surprise, the plane that we were supposed to board did arrive. All of the passengers got off, and we finally boarded even though more flights were being cancelled.

I said to Gail, "This is not going to be good."

The plane taxied out to the runway at LaGuardia, and we sat there for hours. Then the plane taxied back to the gate, and we all had to get off. They then had us board the plane again, and it taxied out to the runway again. I even talked to the pilot, who assured me that he was from Chicago and he was flying this plane home that night no matter what.

We sat on the runway again and waited for a long time. Finally, the plane taxied back to the airport gate, and they had us wait there to board again. Then they finally made the fucking announcement that the flight was cancelled. It was so late at this point, and I couldn't believe they did that to us.

Everyone, including me, was furious and yelling, except a woman close by. She had what looked like twin daughters about seven or eight years old. One had a cap on her head and the mother was carrying a bag with the St. Jude's Children's Hospital logo on it. St. Jude's is for very sick kids, many with terminal illnesses.

This situation of the delays didn't even faze this woman; she must have had real problems and this wasn't even on the scale. She wasn't yelling and just waited patiently with her girls and I just kept thinking about her.

They told all of us on the flight to be back at the airport to take a six in the morning flight to Chicago. As mad as I was, I just kept thinking about that mother; my silly problem was just an inconvenience. Gail and I had a hard time finding hotel rooms since, by this point, it was late and everything was booked.

We made so many calls and finally found a hotel that had a two-room suite, which turned out to be a misnomer. We should have known better, but we had no other choice. We didn't even ask how much it cost.

When we got to the hotel, there was no real lobby since it was under construction, so we couldn't actually see what the hotel was like. Gail got the keys, and as we approached our hotel room, we saw that the door was metal and had dents like it had been kicked in many times.

Gail and I went in and realized that we wanted to spend as little time in that room as possible. We went to dinner and stayed there. We were the last to leave the restaurant. I think we got back at around two-thirty in the morning and had to leave the hotel at four-fifteen. That was more time than anyone should ever have had to spend in that "hotel." I don't even remember how much it cost.

When we got to LaGuardia and were waiting with all the same people as yesterday, I noticed the lady with the two girls again. As tired as I was, she must have been exhausted. She just kept going, and her girls seemed so well behaved. She wasn't complaining like all of the other road-warrior travelers who were threatening the airline and just behaving badly.

Having so many frequent flier miles from all of the travel, I was upgraded to business class. I asked the flight attendant to ask the mother if she or one of her daughters wanted my seat. That it was the least I could do. She declined as she wanted them to all be together and she had the flight attendant thank me for my offer. I was starving but asked the flight attendant to give my business class meal to her and her daughters as the regular cabin didn't get any food. I was so hungry, but that, too, was the least that I could do.

The experience was humbling and it helped make me a better person. All of the road-warrior business travelers were being assholes, and I had become more like them. I flew so much and presumed I was entitled to everything. How could any delay possibly happen to me?

All the way back to Chicago, I thought that this was just not the type of person I wanted to be. I was so angry and tired all of the time because of the travel back and forth between Chicago and New York—I just didn't want to do it anymore. And I was always sick with a sore throat or cold from being tired and around sick and obnoxious travelers all the time.

I made a decision on that flight. It was going to be very risky and with no backup plan. I was going to quit my high-paying job.

After another few months, the midyear bonuses were paid. I was always waiting and chasing to get a bonus. It was a game. I waited two days for the check to clear and walked into Bonnie's office and said, "I resign. I don't want to do it anymore. I'll work through any transition that you need."

She appreciated that.

About thirty minutes later, she came into my office and said, "I have an idea. We don't want to lose your legal skills, so you should consider being our outside counsel. You can keep your same office in Chicago and administrative person, and we will be your client three days a week and sometimes more."

Without another plan, I said, "Let's give it a try."

So, I dusted off The Global Capital Group Ltd. and got it going again. It was good as they loved my work and I didn't have to deal with the travel or the firm politics any more being on my own badge again.

CHAPTER TWENTY-SIX
GLOBAL IS GLOBAL

My consulting arrangement was going well, and I had done a bunch of projects to eliminate legal and compliance backlogs at Scotland International Bank. I was glad to be on my own badge, and I wasn't leaving it again. And then another assignment came.

A friend of mine had recommended me to an industry colleague, David Reed, to do some legal and regulatory consulting for his firm. I had no idea at the time how big this was going to be. He was the new general counsel of a financial services firm, International Financial, with offices around the globe. Although David had a lot experience at this level, he couldn't be everywhere.

"Are you up for an assignment in Madrid? We have some regulatory issues there, and we need your help now," he said.

I jumped at the chance. "I'll leave as soon as you want me to."

It ended up being a sensitive securities trading matter, and it was fascinating. Before jetting off to Madrid, I went to the New York office down on Wall Street to meet with the executives there and the legal and compliance people. I liked all of them, and it had a good vibe.

After visiting New York, I went back to Chicago to pack for a month and left for Madrid. I landed there over the weekend and got to the office first thing that Monday morning. I was escorted to what would be my temporary office. All of that had been arranged beforehand since they wanted me to get to work on the matter without delay. It was like being parachuted in for a special secret operation.

I met with the senior people there, not knowing what their information level was. It was tricky stuff. The gal who headed the office, Sally

Buckingham, ended up being a good gal, and I liked her. She was straightforward and ready to provide any help that she could.

I started digging into the trade data and transactions that were the subject of my assignment and looking at what the legal and compliance obligations were. It didn't take me long to figure out the requirements, but the transactions were not straight forward. In fact, they were very opaque to me. In the past, like when I worked with the guys who spoke Russian, when I ran into transactions that were not so obvious, that was usually a tip and meant there was maybe something fishy.

A particular trading desk, at the Madrid office, was made up of some German guys doing what seemed to be illegal trades in German government bonds. After a thorough review on my part and with the help of senior management of the firm, it was determined that these traders had to leave the firm because the conduct may have been illegal. Even bigger, the matter had to be reported to the local criminal authorities. I never knew what happened as a result as all of that is kept confidential by the authorities.

David asked me to stay in Madrid for a little bit longer to look at some compliance and regulatory structures and make any recommendations that I thought would be useful. I found that fascinating too. It was easy to do that and to be helpful.

I spent a little more than four weeks in Madrid. I was at the airport heading back to Chicago when David called again.

"I need you in Hong Kong."

Again, I jumped at the chance. "When?"

"Immediately."

I did get to go back to Chicago for a few days to pack. He didn't specify what the issue was, but he wanted me to be out in Hong Kong for a few weeks. I didn't mind this. My former firm, Lange and Anderson, had an office there, and I liked Hong Kong with all of its history. It had such a cosmopolitan buzz.

I didn't know it at the time, and neither did David, but I would end up spending the better part of a year in Asia mostly based in Hong Kong. He wanted me to look into a particular matter involving an equity trading desk at the firm's offices in Hong Kong. After that, he wanted me to give an assessment of the legal and compliance processes and procedures and whether improvements could be made.

I thought that was smart on his part since he was still relatively new to the organization and buried in the U.S. stuff and didn't want too much time to go by. I was thrilled to get to do something this interesting.

I flew business class and left Chicago over the weekend so I could get to Hong Kong Sunday night to be in the office first thing Monday morning.

I was prepared and studied the materials that I would need on the flight over. It was tiring, and upon arriving at the hotel, I could only get a few hours of sleep until it was time to go to the office. I didn't have it bad, though. I was staying at the Four Seasons in Hong Kong, which was rather luxurious. They had expensive linens and fresh exotic fruit in my room every day, so I wasn't feeling sorry for myself this time for the travel stuff.

I met with the senior people there and the legal and compliance people on that Monday. The guy who headed the office was Bob Causaway. I did not have a good vibe from him. He was very smart and realized I was like the spy from the home office and likely nothing good would come of that for him. That was not my intention at all, but I would have felt the same if the roles had been reversed.

I quickly got down to work. I talked to Helene Collins, who headed the legal department for Asia, and she was based in Melbourne. We hit it off right away and I realized what a gem they had in her as she was bright and tried to keep everyone on the straight and narrow.

Helene shared her thoughts of who was slippery and who was not, and I later realized that she was so spot on. To this day, although we are oceans away, I consider her and her husband Matt to be close friends. We don't get to speak much, but when we do, it is like no time has passed.

The matter at hand was another one that was not straightforward. The law was, but the transactions weren't. When things are not straightforward, once again my instinct tells me that there is a reason and it usually wasn't a good one. This matter was deep and complex, and to my surprise, I had never seen trades like this before.

There was a desk that traded Asian bonds and was headed by Lee Tan, a guy who seemed slippery to me. I thought maybe I could corner him with questions.

"What are these trades all about? Can you explain them to me?"

He gave me answers that didn't make any sense. After a lot of help from the super smart head compliance guy, Kevin Stanley, it looked like this guy and some others working at different financial firms in Hong Kong were actually front running the Hong Kong government's trades. I couldn't believe it, and they were getting away with it.

I recommended to management that these guys had to leave the firm as these trades might be illegal. Management agreed with my recommendation.

I was very nervous during that time and kept looking over my shoulder in the office and outside of it. I was paranoid because I was oceans away from everyone, alone, and working on some supersensitive stuff. I thought some of these guys might actually try to have someone physically hurt me. That might have been paranoid on my part, but I couldn't be sure that I was safe. I couldn't wait to get home to Chicago.

Part of the assignment was to also look at the compliance program and provide suggestions and recommendations as necessary. The people there were very good, but another set of eyes can sometimes help identify ways to make things better from a compliance perspective.

David liked my recommendations and asked me to stay and help implement them. This was going to be a longer assignment than I had expected, but it was fascinating, and I was staying at the Four Seasons, eating exotic fruit after work and on the weekends. So, except for missing my nephews, it was pretty good.

Then David asked me, as part of the assignment, to go to the office in Mumbai. I had never been to India and had heard mixed things about it. Thankfully, that trip thankfully was only going to be for one week. I didn't want to be there any longer, not knowing what to expect.

I was back in Chicago, and before going to India, I went to get the necessary immunizations to avoid getting sick during international travel in that area of the world. The nurse even suggested a rabies shot. I laughed and declined that one since I was going to be in the hotel and the firm's offices. I later realized that I should have listened to them.

My flight arrived at night in Mumbai, and the airport was crazy. There were so many people and nothing seemed to be organized, which of course didn't help, being so tired. I went out to where the car services were, and luckily, there was a man with a sign that had my name on it. Whew. We went to the car, which was a nice white Mercedes that the hotel had sent to get me. I thought, "Okay, maybe this isn't going to be so bad."

When we left the airport, it wasn't like any highway that I had ever seen before. Nobody was using lanes and it was a free for all. There were taxis, bikes, rickshaws, cars, and about anything else on the same highway, which was mostly a dirt road. We got off the "highway" and drove in what looked more like a city. The driver started to slow down and turned into a driveway. I was scared because I didn't see the hotel name. The automatic gates pulled open and he pulled in and stopped the car. The gates closed behind.

The car was surrounded by armed guards and two big scary-looking dogs. The driver got out and was talking to the guards.

What had I gotten myself into? I was definitely out of my league here.

I stayed sitting in the back of the car since they had guns, and I wasn't sure what I was supposed to be doing.

The driver then lifted the hood of the car, and the guards inspected it. They looked under the car with the dogs too. I realized they were bomb-sniffing dogs. They did the same for the trunk of the car. After all that was done, he said it was all good and escorted me to the hotel lobby. He was not the least bit fazed by any of this, but I was beside myself.

I didn't feel safe at this point, so I stayed at the hotel that night and didn't venture out. The next day, a car picked me up to take me to the firm's office. The roads were dirt and I could see the buses that people were riding in didn't have windows or maybe they were all open. These looked like hardworking people getting to their jobs and it didn't faze them to have open windows and all of the dust. I guess they had gotten used to it.

The offices were not far from where they filmed parts of the movie *Slum Dog Millionaire*. There was so much poverty everywhere, and that is still memorable and sad to me. I was looking forward to getting to the office since it was called the Modern Building and presumed that it was some luxurious building in Mumbai. The car pulled into the lot and stopped in front of the building to let me out.

I thought that the driver must have been mistaken and said, "Sir, I'm going to the Modern Building."

"This is it," he said.

"You've got to be kidding."

He shook his head and I got out of the car.

I took the elevator and even that was odd to me because it was on the outside of the building and parts of it were open. I went to the reception area and waited to be escorted to where I would be working. They had designated a conference room for me to work in, and they said it is the one used by visiting regulators and the auditors. It was cobalt blue, a strange choice for a business office. I should have known something was up.

I met with the two most senior guys of the firm, Phupinder Bombay and Sandy Dalal, and the compliance guy, Mahim Nana, and got right to work. By the middle of the day, I was literally nauseated and sick to my stomach and had a headache too. I had only eaten at the hotel the night before and only drank bottled water so I didn't think it was food poisoning, certainly not yet. There was some strange odor in the conference room that was overwhelming, but I wasn't sure what it was. I did my best and made it through the day but felt sick.

The next day, the same thing happened, so I went straight to Phupinder.

"There is a problem here. There is an overwhelming smell in the conference room and it is making me sick."

"Really?" he said, sounding surprised.

He had the maintenance guy put a fan in the room, which helped for a short while, and then the same nausea and headaches came back. By the middle of the day, I was sick to my stomach. This happened every day, and I couldn't wait to get out of there and on the plane back to Chicago.

Months later, someone from another office of International Financial told me that the room was filled with mold and that was where they put the visiting auditors and regulators so they wouldn't stay long. That was clever and effective. Phupinder and Sandy were as smart and slick as they came. I left after the week was over, and although David wanted me to go back to Mumbai for another month, I vowed to never return.

I was back at the Mumbai airport, and again it was crazy. I couldn't wait to get on the plane. Oddly, the planes left in the middle of the night. We boarded, and I needed as much wine as I could drink to get over that trip. The plane took off for Chicago, and I was glad to be heading home.

Despite the niceties in Hong Kong, I missed my nephews. Don't get me wrong, the country was beautiful and I had done all the fascinating stuff—the outdoor markets and the boat trips to the nearby islands. It was time for me to go home.

David and the others in management wanted to make my role permanent, but I wasn't interested in living in Hong Kong on a full-time basis. I was missing too many weekends already with Ryan and Dan and wanted to end the arrangement. Many of the people there were great but the trips back and forth, twenty hours door-to-door, were tough to do even though I was sipping champagne and eating hot fudge sundaes on the planes.

There was one week, before all of this ended, when the CEO of the whole company, Ralph Orchard, was going to be in the Hong Kong office. Not to my surprise, the head of the office, Bob, thought he had made sure that I didn't know he was coming. Nice try pal. I had a secret meeting all planned in advance by Ralph far from the office at a luxury hotel restaurant.

It was only the two of us, and he wanted my candid views about how things were being handled by senior management in Asia and the head of the Hong Kong office in particular. I recommended that Bob should leave the firm. I didn't like how he handled inquiries with the regulators and he was, in my opinion, trying to be too clever with them. Ralph followed through on my recommendation and Bob left.

CHAPTER TWENTY-SEVEN

THE MONKEYS

One Friday afternoon while I was in Hong Kong, one of the business guys, Marty Lantau, asked, "What are you doing this weekend?"

"Nothing, really. I don't have any plans."

"I have a suggestion for you. If you like the outdoors, you should go hiking on the paths at McGrady Park. You have to bring your own water and snacks since there aren't any once you start on the path," he said.

"That sounds fantastic," I said.

It seemed like a great way to spend part of the weekend, although I did wonder why he was being so nice to me. I should have known better.

I got up early on Saturday and wore light clothes since the temperatures and humidity there were scorching hot. I filled my water bottle and brought a plastic bag with an apple and a pack of crackers as he had suggested.

I took a taxi to the entrance of the park, and it looked nice. There were a few other people around, but it wasn't crowded. I hate crowds, so this was going to be good day. There were two paths, a short one and a longer one, and I picked the longer one. I was looking forward to this and didn't want to rush it.

As I was starting on the path by myself, and about a half mile down, I saw a monkey. He was standing right in the middle of the path, staring at me. I thought how cute since there weren't monkeys in Chicago except at the zoo. I did always think that the monkeys at the zoo were very smart. I took out my Blackberry to take a picture for Ryan and Dan. As I snapped the shot, I noticed that he was coming toward me and getting closer.

This wasn't cute anymore, and before I knew it, something pulled my arm. I was scared to death and screamed and saw that the monkey in the middle of the path was closing in, but worse, there were two others right by my side. I screamed again and was shaking. Then one of them ripped the bag out of my hand and my purse went with it. I screamed again. They left my side, and another hiker quickly came to my aid. He didn't speak English, but I motioned what had happened.

The monkeys had luckily dropped my purse a few feet away or I would have been stuck there with no money, no identification, and no way back. He retrieved my purse, and I thanked him again and again. I got the heck off that path and was never going back again.

I found the first taxi I could and jumped in. I told the taxi driver what had happened. He said they probably smelled the crackers or apple and they'd do anything for food. I was still shaking when I got to my room, and it took a while for me to calm down.

I had been mugged by three monkeys. They were strong and weren't small.

When I got to the office on Monday, Marty stopped by to check in.

"How was it?" he asked.

"It was nice," I replied and then decided to ask what had been on my mind. "Did you know that they have dangerous monkeys there?"

He smiled. "Oh, those. I probably should have told you about them."

He seemed pleased with himself.

Did he really try to get me seriously harmed? Was he that dangerous? I was definitely not going to take any more suggestions from him and watched him closely after that. Thankfully, he found another job at a different firm a few months later, so he left.

Although many of the people in the offices around the globe were nice, there were also a bunch of whackadoos. I had had enough of them and this international traveling. I went back to Chicago and told David that I didn't want to go back to Asia anymore. I think he was disappointed but realized that I missed my family and had been away too much.

I did some work for David when I was back in Chicago and also picked up another two clients. I was working six days a week in my legal and regulatory consulting practice and making plenty of money. I always kept Saturdays open and spent them with Ryan and Dan. This was a good gig, and I was going to keep it going. Always better to be on my own badge.

CHAPTER TWENTY-EIGHT

THE BEAR

Things were going well in my consulting business. Then one day, out of the blue, a friend of mine, Mary, called and said, "Hey, I know of a position to be the chief compliance officer of a pretty large mutual fund complex. You have any interest?"

I knew nothing about this area of law but thought that maybe I should try it so I said, "Yes, thanks a lot."

By this point, I had figured out mergers, rocket man, securities, internal investigations, and a whole host of other things never having done them before, so I thought how hard could this be. She passed my name along to the fund complex, and surprisingly, the recruiter for the position called me.

At the time, the Securities Commission had imposed a new rule that mutual fund complexes and their trading advisors had to have a chief compliance officer. It was a huge deal since many of the fund complexes had gotten into a whole bunch of trouble doing illegal acts and several were paying in the hundreds of millions of dollars in fines. And mutual funds were supposed to be safe investments for regular people and for their retirement funds.

The Securities Commission wanted each fund to have a chief compliance officer reporting directly to the board of directors of the funds and to keep them on the straight and narrow. I thought that part would be right up my alley.

I met with the recruiter, who was impressed with my background. With so many of the fund complexes looking for people to hire for these roles, I thought the recruiter must be desperate as my background wasn't exactly a fit. Although I had deep experience in derivatives, and now securities, I had no direct mutual fund compliance background. I didn't exaggerate my experience and have never done that.

The recruiter then scheduled a meeting for me to meet with the board members. There were five of them, and most were very accomplished high-profile people in Chicago. Three of them, I liked a lot, but two, I didn't. Eventually, it was mutual, with the two of them hating me.

They were all impressed with my background. Again, there must not have been enough qualified people to go around for all of these open slots. The recruiter offered me the job, and I vigorously negotiated my agreement. I had done enough employment agreements to know the trap doors and games that could be played and that they were severance agreements in disguise. And I knew the game.

I also negotiated so that I could continue to have my consulting business on the side so long as it didn't interfere with my role. I didn't think anyone would ever agree to that, but they did. We finally agreed on the terms and I had a start date.

Before beginning in this new job, I used the time to read the laws and rules that applied, the current legal cases, and what the funds were doing to get into trouble. The laws were short and mostly straightforward compared to those for derivatives, so luckily it wasn't that hard for me.

I was nervous starting, thinking that some of the people who worked there would realize that I didn't know that much about mutual funds. I figured that there must be more to know than what I had read and just didn't know it yet. While the position reported to the board, I was actually an employee of the bank that sponsored and was the administrator for the funds. Their logo was a big mean-looking bear.

So I was in the building as an employee of a bank that I didn't work for. It was more like me being a spy on them and they had to pay me, give me an office, and mostly whatever I wanted. It was an odd role and structure, but that was how the rule made it. It worked out well for me and not so much for them.

On the first day, I went to their offices on North Dearborn Street and met the head of the mutual fund group at the bank, Dick Rush. I did not have a good vibe for him, and I had been in my career long enough to know that my instincts were right. Dick showed me to my office, which was away from where the fund group was located and where I couldn't see, hear, or run into them.

I thought, "Are you seriously going to play this game with me?" It was an interior office with no windows and insulting to someone with my experience and credentials. And the office had no computer. Dick said they had ordered it, but it had not come yet. I think it took two weeks to get the computer.

Nobody was doing anything to get me up and running any time soon. Well, as always, nobody fucks with a Flaherty, and when someone does, a return in kind or more is in order. I was going to be the most diligent chief compliance officer that mutual fund complex would ever have. Nothing less would do.

After a few weeks, it became clear to me that I knew at least—and in most cases, more than—what they did about mutual funds. My background provided the practical experience of knowing how the securities are bought and sold for the funds. And when I was in New York working on Wall Street, I had learned about foreign exchange rates, which would become relevant too. I wasn't stupid in math like they thought I was in the first grade in the D track.

I was beginning to feel a lot better about my ability to do well in the role. I kept in touch with the board and everyone seemed pleased. But I was sick of the dark interior office and decided to move. I went into the nearby conference room every day and took it over. It was right where all of the people in the mutual fund area worked. I put myself right in the middle of all of it, with my laptop and documents that I would be using and any other materials needed.

At the end of each day, I would put it all back in my office and lock the door. It was entirely possible that Dick might have gone into my office after I had left to snoop around to see what I was up to. Since they weren't telling me anything about what was going on with the mutual funds, I wasn't telling them anything about what I was working on. That part was going to be some fun.

The conference room was spacious and bright. It would do fine and was more in line with what I thought I should have. Everyone started to get used to my being in there and Dick finally had someone put an electric outlet in there for me and I thought that was progress.

I developed the compliance program from scratch identifying all of the areas, subject to change, to be looked at to see whether they were in compliance with the requirements or hiding problems and illegal trades. I have to say that if I were Dick I would not have liked me in this role. I could figure stuff out without their help and they were always on edge. That made me realize, all the more, that I needed to look wide and deep.

Very quickly it became clear to me that there were some illegal activities and it was not hard to find them. The first one was within a few weeks of starting the job. Dick approved what was called a late trade. The trade was for a very prominent family in Chicago. A late trade happens after the market closes and trades cannot be accepted. Dick had signed off on the trade. One of the gals who worked there, Amanda Lake, who was really smart, brought it to my attention, and I appreciated that she and I were going to get along well.

I marched into Dick's office and said, "Can you explain this to me because I'm confused."

I wasn't confused at all.

He gave me some generic bullshit answer, so I walked out. I called one of the members of the board and quickly arranged a conference call with all of them.

I was very new at this job and they didn't know me well, but I told them, "Dick has approved a late trade in the large equities mutual fund. That is against the rules."

"How do you know that? Are you sure?" one of the said.

I didn't say that Amanda came to me as I didn't want to get her in trouble if they didn't like her or me.

"I was reviewing some trades and this one came to my attention. And yes, I'm sure."

They asked me who the trade was for and I told them.

The general counsel for the bank, Patrick Lincoln, had heard that I told the board members the name of the family for whom the trade was done. He called me and said, "That is a violation of confidentiality and you can be fired for it."

I was worried and called my brother and asked, "What I should do?"

"When you don't know if you're right or wrong, you have to act like you're twice as right," he said.

I thought that was good advice, so with confidence, I called Patrick.

"I'm right and you're wrong." Holding firm, I continued, "And you shouldn't be threatening me because that could be an illegal act on your part."

He hung up the phone and raced to the floor where my office was and came in apologizing and trying to be nice to me. I let the matter go but knew I had to be on the lookout for him too.

Then after another few weeks, I came to realize that there were more illegal acts. Dick and his crack crew had permitted market timing in several of the mutual funds. Market timing is against the rules. It is when an entity times their trades to take advantage of the other investors. Dick left the bank soon after that.

I explained to the board what had happened and that the bank should have to pay back into the mutual funds the amounts that had damaged the other investors. The board agreed.

Before I knew it, there was another problem. Mutual funds have different classes of shares and the investors are charged different fees. They were charging one class of shares too many fees for fewer services, and I thought that was against the law too. This one was big.

Once again, I explained the situation to the board and recommended that the bank repay the amounts back to the investors. The bank was furious and went to the board to try to get me fired. One of the board members had called to tell me. He was so ethical. The other two that I didn't like were likely in on trying to get me fired. They must have finally figured that if I left, it would be a red flag to the Securities Commission, so they backed off.

I kept going and was getting better and better at this stuff. The outside lawyer for the funds, Lisa St. Clair, said that I had a nose for this investigative stuff and she was right. I assumed that if something had been done illegally, I had to find it. It was a game for me, and I found it very interesting, although I don't think it was as much fun for them. I think even the two board members who didn't like me were hoping that my skills would fade, but they kept getting stronger as I met each new challenge head on.

I had only one person assigned to me, Amanda. She was a smart gal with an accounting background and was good at Excel and data. We were a perfect team. I had the theories and we both tried to prove or disprove them. Either way, it was okay as the important thing was figuring out if something had gone off the rails; we were mostly right that it had. Even though Amanda was an employee of the bank, she enjoyed working with me.

The administrative assistant to Dick, Janice Randolph, didn't have much to do when he left the bank. So, I said to the bank's management that I would be glad to have her work with me. I didn't expect to get much out of Janice, but Amanda and I had a lot of work to do and any help would be welcome.

I had observed that, when Dick was there, she did what was given to her and nothing more. She didn't seem at all enthusiastic about her job. Janice wasn't a college graduate and was a bit rough coming from a dangerous neighborhood in Chicago. I always thought that she carried a gun for protection.

When she started working with me, before she began an assignment, I explained what we were trying to do overall. Then for each assignment, I explained to Janice her role and how it was going to help. I also explained what Amanda was working on. I made it feel like a team as that is how I like to work. Janice rose to the challenge and completely changed her attitude.

She became interested in the job and worked so hard to help. It was amazing to see how she had been taken for granted and needed someone to recognize that she was smart and could contribute to the work. I think maybe she reminded me of myself when I was just looking for someone to give me a chance.

When she got it wrong, as we all do with something new, I explained each step to Janice and told her to give it another try. I didn't take it from her and just give it to Amanda. With this approach, I could tell that it gave her more confidence in her skills and her ability to succeed. That was all she needed, which she hadn't been getting there before.

As we dug deeper into the work, I noticed a bunch of times when all of those working at the bank in the mutual fund area would be out of their offices and nowhere in sight.

Ah, they must be meeting without me to discuss what I am up to.

That made me smile.

If they had included me, I would have told them step by step what I was looking at and working on. I had nothing to hide and always wanted to be transparent with them. That definitely only went one way.

One day, Janice brought into the conference room a piece of paper and closed the door.

"I've been able to get the schedule of all of their meetings without you and it's intentional. They're meeting behind your back all the time and you should know about it," she said.

It was as I had suspected, but I didn't take the piece of paper.

"Thank you, Janice. I appreciate you wanting to level the playing field for me. But I won't look at it. If I take that piece of paper, I will be no better than they are and I have to play this the fair way."

Janice respected that, although I think she was still on the lookout anyway.

I was reviewing some sensitive areas of the management of the funds, and there was a lot of tension. The people who worked there said hello to me if they walked past me in the hall but that was it. They didn't want me there and it was obvious. I was fine with that and didn't let it bother me. I was there to do a job for the board and the shareholders of the mutual funds. Then one day, I was in for a shock.

I was in the conference room and Janice was in there with me. I was sitting at the table and she was standing beside me since we were going over some work. Out of the blue, from the building right across the street, there was a strobe light or laser and it was aimed directly at the center of my forehead. Janice dropped to the ground; where she lived, she knew trouble when she saw it. She was startled and afraid, and I was too. We both got out of that room fast.

"What the fuck was that?"

Was there a reasonable explanation, or was someone targeting to shoot, harm, or threaten me? This was no random accident. The laser was pointed directly at my head. Was I getting too close to some bad stuff they didn't want me to uncover?

I didn't want to be paranoid, but under the circumstances, I didn't know what to think.

I debated what to do, so I thought about it and decided that there should be a police report. If I reported it to the bank, they might not take it seriously. And maybe it was someone there that had arranged to scare me anyway.

Were they trying to scare me so I would quit my job? Or could it be even worse?

I called the police and they came. Janice was there to back me up. I described to the two police officers which floor and office from across the street that laser came from. They took the report and then went across the street to the building to check it out.

They came back and said, "The office was empty and locked, and there was no sign of anyone in it."

Then whoever did that, were they watching me and saw that I had called the police?

I didn't know what to do, but I went back to the conference room to work. I didn't want to go back to the other dark office with no window. I wasn't going to let them scare me. So, I kept going.

I worked at it harder even though there was potentially a target on my head and maybe my back. There were so many recommendations to the board that the bank pay back to the shareholders any amount that harmed them. In all, based on my super sleuth work with Amanda and Janice, the bank had to repay over fifty million dollars back to the mutual funds.

I had a conversation with the temporary head of the mutual funds, Toby Bryn.

"You know that I'm not leaving. And why did the bank ever get into this business anyway? It wasn't ever properly staffed, and this stuff is very technical," I said. "The bank should get out of this business and transfer the funds to another fund complex."

It would be good for me too, but I didn't mention that as I would get paid out early on my employment agreement and not have to finish the two years. When I suggested to get out of all of this, his eyes lit up like a Christmas tree. He knew that I was right and that it was the only way to graciously get out of that business and get rid of me at the same time.

The bank decided that this was a good idea and started searching for a group to transfer the funds to. It took months, but they found an organization that would get them out of this mess and away from me. The organization purchasing the funds wanted to interview and interrogate me as they saw all of my recommendations. I told them to fuck off as I didn't work for them and was never going to.

It took a while for the deal to close, and I kept going to the very end. I never let up and did my best every day. I did keep in touch with Janice for a while; I recommended her for several jobs, and she got them.

On the last day, I got paid the remaining amount on my employment contract, which was a good thing for me. That was my only mistake—I didn't think to tell the executives to sell the funds sooner.

CHAPTER TWENTY-NINE

BACK AGAIN

I went back to my legal and regulatory consulting business, and it was going great. I was happy in Chicago, and there was no reason to make any changes. As a consultant, I didn't get involved in any company politics and I produced quality legal and regulatory work. Everyone was happy. They got my work, I got paid. Well, that was about to change.

One of my clients, Scotland International Bank, needed a global head of compliance and anti-money laundering. They were a large organization in the financial markets, and I knew their business well as I had previously been their general counsel in the U.S. and then their legal consultant. They liked me and I liked them.

The general counsel at Scotland International Bank, Bill Menard, approached me about the global role and I said that I wasn't interested, and I meant it. I had gone off my own badge multiple times and always wanted to get back to it. It was so much simpler without the politics. I also didn't want to give up my consulting business since it could be hard to get it up and running again. Bill approached me again, but my answer was still the same.

Then he came back a third time. He was persistent.

I thought about it and said, "Well, I might be interested."

It is one role that I had not held before. I had been the general counsel several times but had not held a big global role. I finally agreed and carefully negotiated my agreement with lots of money and protections for me if it didn't work. At this point in my career, I was much better at negotiating employment contracts for myself, having been through mergers, takeovers, and all that stuff.

After the ink was dry on the agreement, I quickly got started as there was a lot to do. I had a team of eighty people in ten countries, and I visited each of the offices. I loved this team. They were all smart, hardworking, and supportive of each other and me. There were a few key positions to fill, and I made good judgments and hired quality people. They were all talented people dedicated to keeping the company out of trouble.

Oh, and we had lots of issues. I was responsible for compliance and anti-money laundering. These areas are highly dependent on regulatory technology tools. We had to work night and day to improve in these areas, and we did.

The company was far behind on compliance surveillance and didn't have all of the right tools, and the regulators were not happy about it. I fought to get increases in my technology budget to help keep the company out of regulatory trouble. I was glad that, at the top, there was a strong commitment to compliance, which is one of the reasons I took the job.

We got right to it and started fixing, enhancing, and expanding surveillance to detect trading abuses and suspicious activities. I worked to pull the group working more as a team rather than silos in each country. We developed a global compliance and anti-money laundering program from scratch, which hadn't formally existed before. The whole team got to have input as we were all going to own it. Everyone was excited and proud, and we implemented it globally. This was the kind of work that I loved to do.

There was one bureaucratic committee, and if a department was going to spend more than $40,000 on a vendor's service, it had to be preapproved. I was on the committee and thought it was useless. My surveillance system was going to cost millions of dollars to get it right, and I didn't have time to waste on this stupid approval process.

Well, I came up with what I thought was a clever idea. I had my technology guy, Alan Lawndale, tell the vendor to bill us for each exchange for surveillance rather than all of them as a whole bill. We had to keep each bill under $40,000. The vendor agreed, and I was getting away with it. I wasn't getting anything out of it but wanted to get the company out of regulatory trouble. The accounting department at our company hated me because the billing was screwed up for years.

Well, one day, my trick was almost blown. I was on another useless call with the committee, and someone from the technology department was talking about an important change to a major system in the firm. I started listening more carefully and didn't like what I was hearing. After understanding what he was talking about, I jumped in.

"You can't do that! You'll interfere significantly with my multimillion-dollar trade surveillance system," I said.

Then all of the people, about twelve of them, went silent.

Then one of them said, "What multimillion-dollar trade surveillance system?"

Oops.

I had to act fast and pretended that there was static on the phone. I said my cell phone was coming in and out, and the street traffic was so loud now. And then I quickly hung up. I sat right there in my office laughing hysterically. I did have Alan go behind the scenes to cover for me and make sure that there was no interruption in our surveillance systems. The two of us were as thick as thieves and still are.

I loved working with my teams of compliance and anti-money laundering folks. And at that point in my life and career, I enjoyed mentoring younger colleagues, which was pretty much everybody. They used to call me Yoda, meaning old wise one. I thought it was funny.

This job was great, and spending lots of time in London and the other cities with parts of the teams there was also fantastic. They were always welcoming and glad to see me. I would walk around to people's desks and be interested with what they were working on.

Nobody on my team was intimidated since I made sure that our group was "flat" from an organization perspective. Everyone got to work, and nobody stood on hierarchy. Even with the big title, I was just one of the gang.

Things were going so well, then I realized that something else was going on. The company was very capital intensive, meaning it takes a lot of money to run something this big. And it wasn't making money.

Oh, here we go again.

The shareholders weren't happy about it and were looking to sell the company, and that was awful. I had stepped away from my consulting to do this, and what was going to happen now? I wasn't worried about me as I had been making New York money in Chicago and saving, but I was worried for all of my young and talented team.

Even though all of this was going on in the background, we forged ahead and kept doing the hard work we were supposed to. We had implemented a ton of technology fixes and tools, hired top talent to review surveillance results, and ran a top-notch compliance and anti-money laundering function.

The executive committee of the company, of which I was a member, was very impressed with what we were doing in the compliance and anti-money laundering space. I tried to be clever and found better ways to use statistics to communicate what we actually did since they didn't fully understand it.

I had another motive too. I was trying to strategically look a few steps ahead. I figured if they were going to downsize the company at some point and cut jobs, I didn't want any cuts in compliance or anti-money laundering.

On a monthly basis, for my presentation at the executive committee meetings, I would list out things like how many regulatory requests we received and had to respond to. There were thousands. The largest number came from the U.S., and we had figured out how to automate many of the responses with minimal staffing input. But there was no reason for me to spell that out to anyone.

Every month, I listed in painful detail the number and types of surveillance alerts that had been reviewed. Those were often more than ten thousand a month. My team was very efficient, and we calibrated the system and had very qualified staff so they could get through them relatively quickly. Once again, there was no reason to highlight that.

Each month, when I gave my compliance and anti-money laundering report at the executive committee, I tried to look tired and overworked. At the end of my report, they were amazed at how much my team could do with such a small staff. They were impressed. They also appreciated that I never asked for more headcount and made do with the staff size that I had. It was actually easy, but there was no reason to be that transparent since I had another reason for what I was doing, and it was to protect the jobs of my team.

As I had suspected, the CEO, Patrick George, came to me and said, "There are going to be staffing cuts, and you have to take your fair share and reduce your team."

I had laid the foundation so well and that wasn't going to happen. There was no way that was I going to cut anyone in my group. I liked all of them too much and we were doing a great job keeping the company in line.

When I met with Patrick, I made him aware that the company might get into trouble with the regulators if we did not have adequate staffing in compliance and anti-money laundering, and it would be on his watch. I also pulled out my trusty statistics that he had marveled at every month.

"Okay, of these thousands of regulatory requests, on an annual basis, which ones should we skip?" I asked. "Should we thumb our noses at the Securities Commission, the Derivatives Trading Commission, the Feds, or should we pick the U.K. regulators to ignore? Or maybe better, the ones in Asia? They are farther away."

He sighed and knew exactly what I was doing, but he couldn't disagree.

My strategy worked. There were cuts almost everywhere else in the company, but none for my compliance and anti-money laundering teams. Several of the other executive committee members were furious since their areas were affected and they had to cut jobs. Too bad, I won and didn't care. My team was fine. But I did feel bad for the other employees who lost their jobs.

We kept delivering great compliance and anti-money laundering work, improving systems. All worked well together. Unfortunately, it became clear that the company was not going to be able to continue as a stand-alone entity. One of the shareholders was going to have to take over and absorb the company. What a bummer. It was so depressing. All of that hard work, gone. And this job that I loved would never be the same.

I thought that it would be particularly tough in the U.S. as these takeovers can be bloody messes and the people who wear the badge of the company that gets taken over are often treated like trash. No matter how good my people were, they weren't going to get the same chance. I thought about getting another job or getting my consulting business back and running, but I wanted to stay through the takeover date to fight for good positions for my team. I wasn't worried about myself, but I was worried about them.

Patrick then told me they wanted me to move to their London office, which was where he was based. There were some nasty politics in the U.S., and I thought some people might have felt like I was a threat to their jobs. I wasn't, but it didn't matter.

The company rented a nice furnished one-bedroom apartment for me for about eight months. It was a near the office and Liverpool Street. I went along but had no intentions of permanently moving there. Ryan and Dan were in Chicago and I wasn't going anywhere. But if they were going to screw me, hey, why not spend a few months in London at their expensive apartment, hanging around London on the weekends?

I had fun and took full advantage knowing this was all very temporary. I went to Buckingham Palace, all of the gardens, and Greenwich, where they actually have a clock to measure Greenwich Mean Time. I went to fancy London business dinners and cocktail parties and had champagne and really enjoyed it.

I also bought lots of new stuff while there, including hand bags, scarves, you name it. I had a theory whenever living in another city. If I was there on a weekend, something new was a must. So I treated myself well. At some point, I did have to get it all back to Chicago, but that was a worry for later.

In August, when I was in London, I had a fancy lunch with Patrick, which included wine. He was a Scottish guy and I liked him. I could tell that something was off, and he seemed a bit nervous for such a confident guy. He was smart and practical too (so, of course, he isn't with the company anymore).

At lunch, we had a candid conversation, and I said I wasn't moving to London. We had lots of wine and discussed my leaving at the end of the year. He also wanted me to leave the company on good terms. He knew that I could land somewhere I could hurt them. And he was so right.

We were working out the terms of my leaving and it was getting contentious since other lawyers on their side from Edinburgh had gotten involved. I called Patrick directly to let him know that it wasn't going well and was going in a bad direction.

I said, "Patrick, I have one question for you."

"What is it, Eileen?"

"Do you want to go to war with me? One answer, yes or no?"

"Absolutely not."

To his credit, he cleared the other lawyers out of the way who were too shortsighted to see my future. Patrick and I, we worked it out. And to this day, I think very highly of him. There were no bad feelings for anyone. And that was a good thing as the lawyers in the Edinburgh office learned within a few months where I was going to work next. I had heard that some of them gasped and swore when they heard where my next job was. I was very happy to hear that. Nobody fucks with a Flaherty.

I was glad after leaving since some of the people in the Edinburgh office were not going to be the type of people that I wanted to work with. I didn't think our ethics would be on the same page. So I was shocked, and shouldn't have been, when I got a call from a former colleague, Cynthia Lexington, to tell me that one of our administrative assistants, Cheryl Hudson, from the Chicago office had been fired.

She was a nice hardworking gal who was a single mother to a daughter and a son. She had some real family issues. Cheryl's husband had recently passed away, and her daughter had a serious illness that must have cost a lot in medical bills. She was totally down on her luck and nothing she had any control of.

She wasn't making a lot, and with what she had on her plate, she couldn't have been saving money. So one day, the human, or better yet, the in-human resources department called Cheryl into an office and said her job was over and outlined what her severance would be. They fired her that day with no notice, and she didn't do anything wrong.

This gal was probably at one of the lowest points in her life. In the meantime, the executives were flying around the world in business class, sipping champagne, but they fired her to save money for the company.

Several of my former team members and I tried to help get Cheryl back on her feet. That was the character of my former team, unlike some in the Edinburgh office. I was glad to not be there anymore. I will never forget what they did to her.

Over the years, as I rose in my career, I had lots of knife fights but always with peers and superiors. I believe a company should never pick on someone who is in a staff position and never anyone who is down on their luck, like that gal was.

For most of the places I have left, I don't think about them anymore. But I think a lot about those people in the Edinburgh office and what they did to Cheryl.

Time will come when payback will be due for what they did to her. And on that day, it will be served cold.

CHAPTER THIRTY

DC AND ME

Although I was glad to be out of the last company and away from the assholes in Edinburgh, I still stayed in touch with many on my team. I think some of them had wished that I would go and take another global role and bring the band back together again. I wish that I could have done that, but it was prohibited for me to try to hire anyone away. I always regretted that as I think we could have done well helping another large organization stay out of trouble with the regulators.

I owed the last organization some consulting for six months, which was mostly good for me. It gave me some breathing room to figure out what I was going to do next. But it was a restless time for me, and no jobs were coming that I wanted. It wasn't about money, but when you have time off that you don't want, and it is the dead of winter, it can be stressful.

Then one day, a friend in Washington, DC, Katie Alexandria, called me and said that there was an open senior position and that I should put in my name for it. The position was director of the Division of Markets and Clearing at the Derivatives Trading Commission. The position was based in DC. I wasn't sure I wanted the position, but I put my name in to see what would happen.

The position was posted to be a merit hire. In that federal organization, the chairman, who is always a presidential appointee, gets to select the division directors, and there are only four of those. They can decide to hire political hacks who may or may not be qualified, or they can post the job and the selected candidate has to be qualified and make it through a rigorous competitive process.

To the credit of Chairman Jonathan Potomac, he decided to post the position based on merit. The following chairman went the political route, which was no surprise to me.

I should have known from the application process that I was not cut out to be a government gal. It was a long, convoluted, and complicated process employing plenty of people because it was a messed-up waste of time. Anyway, I got through it and had heard that there were a lot of candidates applying for the job.

Months went by of not hearing anything, and then I did.

A nice woman, Beth, called and said, "Can you come to Washington for an interview with the screening committee?"

I agreed and made my flight reservation right away.

I was starting to get excited about a big job in DC and that maybe there was a chance of getting it.

I flew there for a day trip and met with the individuals on the committee. They wanted someone who was qualified and knew the industry well. I thought that the interviews went well as this derivatives stuff had been my space now for decades. More waiting and more hearing nothing. Then, when I was at an industry conference in DC in early May that year, I got a call from Beth.

"Can you come by to meet with Chairman Jonathan Potomac?" she asked.

I went, and he was a bit difficult to read. He said I was obviously qualified, and then the conversation became more relaxed.

Jonathan asked me, "What is the biggest risk in the industry?"

I said, "There are certain known operational points of failure in the electronic trading systems, and even though there are backups, the markets would be severely disrupted if a failure were to occur."

"Nobody has ever said that out loud to me before," he commented.

"Because it's the dirty little big secret, and nobody wants to admit," I said.

Jonathan seemed impressed.

After leaving that long day, on the flight home, I was cautiously optimistic that maybe I would get the job. Many more weeks went by in the government waiting game, and then the call from Jonathan came.

"I'm offering you the job, and I hope that you'll accept it."

"I can't wait to start," I said.

How thrilling to be going to DC to have this big cool job. And the timing was right as Ryan and Dan were in late high school and college and buried in their own stuff. This was my time. Eileen from Burbank, who was in the dummy track for twelve years, was going to be a division director, hired on merit in Washington, DC.

I had plenty to do in a short period of time as they wanted me to start in a few weeks. I took a two-day trip there to try to find an apartment. The income taxes in DC were ridiculous so I focused on Arlington, Virginia. It was green there, and a lot of high rises had a gym, concierge, and other fancy stuff. The apartments weren't cheap, but at least you got something for your money.

I killed myself those two days that I couldn't move by the end of each. I settled on the first apartment I visited and thought that it would be fine. It was a one-bedroom apartment with a small balcony. I asked the property manager if this was on a quiet side of the building since I am a light sleeper. He assured me that it was. I would have to take the Metro system to get to work every day, but it was only four stops, so I could manage it.

I decided that I was not going to move any furniture to that apartment and would get what was needed there. I did order a bed over the phone from the 1-800 bed people to be delivered the day that I arrived. I also packed seven boxes of clothes, kitchen, bedding, and bath stuff. It would be plenty to start with and I could always add more later. It was all part of the big DC experience and adventure.

CHAPTER THIRTY-ONE
MOVING AGAIN

My new big job in Washington, DC, was to start the third week of August in 2016. I was so excited about this, never having done Washington policy before. And to be able to do that in the industry where I had worked for thirty-one years was exciting. It felt so amazing that they picked me—and they picked me on merit and my qualifications. I was not some political appointment, which often puts unqualified people in important roles who then achieve very little.

I was keeping my Chicago condo and going to live in the apartment that I had rented on the trip a few weeks earlier. I had a Wednesday morning flight and was hoping to arrive in time to meet the bed delivery people. The flight was on time. So far, so good.

But I was worried about my seven boxes. What if they didn't get there? What would I do with only the few things with me on the plane?

It was a sunny day, and I arrived by cab to my new apartment building. When I showed up, the woman at the reception desk, Molly, was lovely and so nice, and it got better as my boxes had arrived.

I got to unpacking the clothes, hanging them up and putting the few kitchen essentials in the cabinets. The bed comforter was so welcome as it was mine from the house where I had grown up in Burbank; I had a suspicion that I would need that comfort at some point.

And then I waited and waited. Where were the 1-800 bed people? When I got hold of them by phone, I heard dreadful words.

"There's no delivery today."

Ugh.

I had no couch, no chair, nothing. I went shopping and bought two pillows and a TV. The guy at the TV store thought that I should buy one with a bigger screen. I told him my criterion was whether I could carry it myself the two blocks to my new apartment.

Buying the smaller screen was smart, and even with that one, I had to stop every twenty feet and put it down as it was so heavy. I kept saying I was gonna make it, and I did. I didn't have a TV stand, so four of the moving boxes would have to serve, and they became the permanent TV stand. Another moving box was the nightstand that would go next to the new bed if it ever arrived. Another moving box was the makeshift dinner eating surface. I would sit on the floor, and the box served as my little dinner table. So far, things were going pretty well, and I had no complaints.

I had two pillows, a TV, and my comforter. The floor was my bed the first night in the apartment. I was exhausted but had to get some food before crashing on the floor. I couldn't find a grocery store, so I went to CVS, which is more of a convenient store than a grocery store. They had cereal and milk, so it was fine. I thought there had to be a grocery store as all of these people in the apartments couldn't be living on food from CVS. I would have to figure that out later.

I couldn't sleep on the floor, and only when exhaustion kicked in was I able to get an hour or two of sleep. Upon waking up, I had such a backache and almost couldn't get up. I rolled on my side and slowly was able to stand up and then get to the gym early that day as I couldn't miss the 1-800 bed people.

I was so glad when they came. I put the bed together and I fell into it to take a break—it was pretty good. Not perfect, but then again, I ordered it over the phone, so it would have to do.

It was Thursday, and my new job was to start on Monday. I was so excited and still had so much to do. I found the house stuff store and got an ironing board and an iron. I had to make multiple trips since that store was about five blocks away and I could only buy what wasn't too heavy to carry.

I did buy a folding snack table on one of my trips and a folding chair on another trip. I was living in luxury now with a chair that I could sit on and a snack table for dining. What more did I need? The whole apartment thing was working out. This was going so much better than when I had moved to New

York. I was tired from all of the trips to the stores, so falling asleep in my new bed was easy. It felt good.

I woke up on Friday without setting the alarm. Time for the gym and then to get to work planning my first day on the new job. The gym thing worked out pretty well too. On most days, there were only a few people and I didn't have to wait for a cardio machine. I showered and decided it was time to practice going on the Metro and how to get to work my first day on the job the following Monday.

The Metro in DC was surprising. The ceilings were amazing, and it was so clean and immaculate. There was no garbage on the ground like in Chicago. I was also impressed with the men who rode the Metro. If a woman got on a train car and all of the seats were taken, the men would offer their seats. How classy they were. I never saw that happen in Chicago or in New York and had been shoved out of the way many times so some guy could get to the seat first.

And there was another observation that surprised me. There were a lot of military personnel taking the Metro as it stopped near the Pentagon before heading into DC. They never took seats. Even if there were open seats. I guess they presumed they could fill up and they didn't want to take a seat that someone else could use. How honorable of those people serving our country.

I got my round-trip train ticket and figured out which side of the tracks would head into DC. The train arrived, and it was a smooth sail. I had used Google Maps to help me figure out how to get to the office. I got there and walked around the Derivatives Trading Commission a few times. I wasn't stalking or anything, but trying to get a sense of what was around. I felt much better that things would be fine on Monday.

I had Saturday and Sunday free and had a great time. On Saturday, I went to the Mall and on Sunday went to the mall. The Mall in DC is the area from the Capitol all the way to the Lincoln Memorial. I enjoyed the monuments and all of the history.

It made me remember when I was in the fifth grade and my parents took my brother and me to DC to see all of the sights. It was an adventure as there was no Google Maps or anything then, and you had to find hotels along the way. I remember seeing the Capitol and the Supreme Court and thinking that

I wanted to go back there one day. DC was like I remembered it with my parents on that family vacation.

On Sunday, I stayed close to the apartment and found the mall about three blocks away. I would definitely be spending a lot of time here. I had my first-day-on-the-job outfit all set and kind of just hung out getting ready for the first day.

On Monday morning, I got up early and headed for the gym to be energized for my first day. I showered and put on my first-day outfit and thought it was stunning. Of course, there was a lot of pink, as that is my signature color. Heading for the Metro, I was a bit nervous, which surprised me since I'd had big jobs before and many of them. But this seemed bigger as it was Washington, DC.

I got to the Metro early, not taking any chances if the system was down or something. It was again a smooth sail, and I got to the building of the United States Derivatives Trading Commission at 2055 M Street.

I still wasn't used to the whole letter and number thing with the streets, and every few blocks there would be a diagonal street with some name like Pennsylvania or New York. God knows where you would end up if you took one of those. I never found an Illinois street, which would have been nice, and probably would have hung around there.

Being early, I didn't enter the building yet and didn't want to look overly anxious, so I walked around the block in amazement that Eileen from Burbank was here. When it was appropriate, I went in and introduced myself to the security guards. To this day, I always remember how nice, alert, and friendly they were.

I was escorted to an area and told that someone would come to get me. And someone did and brought me to my office on the 8th floor. There it was, a plaque with my name on it, which was another wow. I thought wow a lot in the beginning, and then later the wows were for other reasons. That morning, there was way too much red tape, more than I would have expected.

My office was interesting, and even though it was not my style, it was impressive. It was very Washington with wood furniture and bookshelves. There was the desk area, a table area, and a meeting area with a couch and chairs. They were covered in a conservative fabric. The décor of the office screamed important official business. I could definitely see myself working in this space.

In the government, different levels of employees get different sizes of offices and types of furniture depending on their position. It is bureaucratic and silly. Since I had a pretty high-level position at this agency, I got this office and furniture. I thought everyone should get the same.

With all of my first-day excitement, what I didn't notice until about a week later was that the carpet was actually filthy although it purportedly had just been cleaned. By whom or what, I thought. And then a few weeks later, I noticed the little roaches dancing in the drawers of my desk. I got to know Toni, the roach exterminator gal, pretty well. She was always crawling on the ground trying to catch them.

The security people at the agency had already taken my fingerprints for a background check weeks before starting the job and, of course, the check came back clean. I wasn't a criminal. On the first day, there were more fingerprints, pictures for a badge, and more paperwork. It was overwhelming, and I wanted to get to work.

It seemed that they had a lot of people on this administrative stuff and each person seemed to only have a single task, although they were all very nice. It was at some point during the first day that I realized, oh my god, I was actually working for the federal government. And some of the stuff maybe shouldn't have surprised me, but they did.

Finally, I was freed from the administrative crap at least for that day. I was the director of the Division of Markets and Clearing at the Derivatives Trading Commission and oversaw the exchanges and clearing organizations in the derivatives markets. Within my division, I had four groups, each led by a deputy director. Three of them, Terry Capitol, Franklin McArthur, and Ethan War, were in DC, and I thought they were great.

We met that afternoon and had a good discussion about what each group did. I knew a lot of this from my positions in the industry, so luckily there wasn't much of a learning curve. Each of the deputies in DC was so enthusiastic about their team and their work, and I was so impressed with them. And while they knew me, they had never worked with me.

Each deputy in DC made it clear that they wanted to work with me and support me. I made it very clear that although pro-business, I would never do anything that would sacrifice customer protections in the markets. That mattered to them and it mattered to me, so I felt so good at the end of the first day that we were going to do great things together.

The first week was about ten hours each day, and it ended up being that way most days. I never got tired of it. And I answered my own phone too, which surprised many people.

After the first week, I still hadn't found the grocery store and was sick of eating cereal every day from CVS. Although the mall had takeout food, I was too tired to walk the extra block each day that first week. That weekend, I had to figure out where the grocery store was hiding. They should have had better marketers.

The first week was kind of a blur, and there was way too much administrative stuff. For most of the week, and the following week, there were groups of people from different areas of the Derivatives Trading Commission who came and presented to me a bunch of stuff. It was too much information. Many of them didn't seem to care if I was taking it in or not, but they could check the box that they had given whatever information they were peddling to the new division director.

There was one group who came to my office to talk about the travel policy of the Derivatives Trading Commission and, in particular, international travel. I think there were four or five of them, and the room was crowded. They quickly covered domestic travel as they wanted to talk about international travel.

"Before we begin on that, I have a question," I said. "I heard that if I travel internationally that I have to fly coach class. Is that correct?"

They said yes with pride.

"Can I use my own frequent flyer miles to upgrade to business class?" I asked.

"No, it isn't allowed."

"Then I guess we can all save this time as I don't need any more information," I said.

They were confused.

"I'm not going to do any international travel," I clarified for them. "I don't do coach anymore for international stuff."

I wasn't a prima donna or anything, but with 1.9 million frequent flyer miles for international travel in business class, I am not flying coach for business at this point in my life. They still wanted to give me their spiel, but I had no interest.

"Let's save the taxpayers the money of going over all of this as it is never going to happen, and let's get back to work."

They looked confused when they left. I was glad they were gone. I wanted to get to work. It took me a while before I figured out that these folks think that attending these meetings IS actually work.

At some point, one group said that I would have to fill out the documentation for a security clearance.

"What is that?"

"With your job, you might get access to high-level confidential information," they explained.

I told them that I had already been fingerprinted not once but twice and that should be sufficient. I wasn't a criminal no matter how many times someone was trying to prove that I was. Although I wasn't interested in participating, it wasn't an option to skip all of that crap.

Apparently, someone in some area of the government, which was never really clear to me, would do a thorough search, reaching back decades and talking to neighbors and so on. The administrative staff said the process can take longer than a year.

"But my merit appointment is only a year, so they'll get the results after I have gone," I said.

"Yes, that is how it works in the government."

I couldn't believe what a waste of taxpayer money this was. Although I wouldn't let this administrative crap dampen my enthusiasm, I couldn't help but constantly question why nobody wanted the processes to be more efficient and cost-effective. People kept saying, "Yep, that's the U.S. federal government." I have a suspicion that exists at a lot of state and city levels too, which disappoints me greatly. Anyway, it didn't get me down since I had too much to do.

On the Monday of the second week of work, I went to bed and was awakened in the middle of the night by a loud, shrill beeping noise. I tried and finally fell back to sleep. The next night, the same thing happened. I got up and realized my side of the building, which I was told was "the quiet side," actually faced a parking lot where dozens of school buses parked. At about three in the morning, they started moving the whole lot of buses. When the buses backed up, they made a shrill beeping noise, which didn't seem to stop.

Ugh, what am I going to do?

I went to work the next day exhausted again and called the apartment manager, Nick, as soon as the office opened.

"If you keep the windows closed and the air-conditioning on, it would be better," he said matter-of-factly.

"Well, that's not happening," I said.

"Okay, you can move to the other side of the building, but a unit wouldn't be ready for two weeks," he informed me.

There was nothing I could do but wait it out and then move. I was beginning to think maybe this is like New York all over again with all the moves.

Then the other shoe dropped, and I sure didn't see this one coming. Before I had accepted the job, I had spoken with Valerie, the staff person in DC responsible for reviewing conflicts of interest. I gave her the information on all of my stock holdings before I ever took the job and asked if there were any issues as it would affect my decision whether to take the job.

"Don't worry, we don't force anyone to sell any of their stocks and we work with people on these matters," Valerie said.

Based on that, I accepted the job.

Now in the second week, and I was tired from little sleep, a group of conflicts people came to give me their spiel. Toward the end of it, they said, "We have to look at your stock holdings."

I could tell that some of them were nervous. I paused and then said, "No, you don't. You've already done that, and I have the emails to prove it."

They all got very quiet and left. I was outraged and didn't know what was going to happen.

How could this be happening now?

A few days later, the general counsel, James Morone, wanted a meeting with me on the topic. I agreed and brought one of my deputies with me, having a sense I needed a witness. His position was that I would have to sell a substantial amount of the stocks.

I could feel my blood pressure escalating.

"That is not happening as Valerie already reviewed my portfolio before I started, and I was told that I would not be required to sell anything."

James, who was a complete weasel, wouldn't acknowledge that.

"I will send you the emails as I have proof," I repeated.

He said again and again, "It doesn't matter."

I continued to correct him. "Oh yes, it does matter."

It was tense. You see the Dow had dropped 2,000 points by now from the time that they said there wasn't a problem and that we could work it out. Now not only did they change that on me without notice, this guy wasn't even acknowledging that his staff person had screwed up. What an asshole.

This back and forth lasted for days, and I wasn't budging. I was called to a meeting with the chairman of the Derivatives Trading Commission, Jonathan, and his chief of staff. He apologized and said that it should not have happened.

"You won't be able to do the job unless you sell the stocks," he said.

It was very upsetting to me, but I kept my cool.

I ended up having to sell the stocks.

What a place, I thought.

And James never apologized for the lack of care of his staff and the personal issues that this caused me. I was then seeing some of the types of people who work in the federal government. Nobody lost their job for this, there were no consequences for them, and there was no accountability.

After another week, I slept in on Saturday and then went to the gym. Then I had to solve the grocery store mystery. I asked Rosie, who was the concierge, if there was a grocery store anywhere close by. She told me it was about five blocks away and how to get there. I was grateful as I never would have found it. It was wonderful and clean and nice people working there. I eventually got to know the fish guy, Lenny, who took good care of me.

On Sunday, I went shopping to the mall, not the other Mall. After the first few weeks, I definitely deserved something new. Eventually, there were so many of those weeks that the stuff from the mall was piling up. At some point, I would have to get all of this stuff back to Chicago, but I so needed those pick-me-ups after each tough week.

I bought about twelve sweaters, six shirts, seven skirts and eleven pairs of shoes. Of course, when the shower gel went on sale I bought fifteen or maybe more. I couldn't help myself as I wanted new stuff each time I finished another week. When I moved back to Chicago it took me nine months to integrate all of this stuff into my closets.

It was a few weeks later when the business manager assigned to my Division, Mike Kingset up a meeting with me to discuss filling the several open positions in my Division. He explained the first open slot and gave me the paperwork to sign to get going on filling. I again realized this is the government and there was unnecessary red tape for everything. Mike asked me to sign the paperwork.

"I first want to evaluate whether we needed to fill the position," I said.

He then went through the other open positions and my response was the same. He was shocked.

"We shouldn't fill open positions unless we need to. This is taxpayer money that pays for staff and we shouldn't be wasting it."

"Mike tried to convince me otherwise, but I wasn't budging.

"You don't understand how the government works. If you don't fill an open position you might lose it. It might get transferred to another Division," he said, nicely.

"What is wrong with that? If my Division doesn't need the position, then it should go somewhere else or be eliminated."

"Mike walked away shaking his head. I felt good about not wasting tax payer money. I learned that I was the only one in the building doing that.

I also learned about a concept that was a new one on me. It's called telework. It is where people get paid and they don't show up for work. They stay home. I had never heard of it before. In the private sector occasionally if someone had a delivery or something coming to their house, they will a little late coming in. Oh, not in the government, people pick which days they will "work from home."

The problem with that is there is no way to know if someone actually worked that day or spent the day walking the dog or shopping. I knew the answer for some people, and I thought it was a sham. I was surprised that people in the private sector didn't know about it or I think they would complain to their congressman.

There were people making $200,000 a year and pretty much working four days a week. I was glad that, although my deputy directors and associate deputy directors and many other members on the team could have taken advantage of the telework policy, they didn't. They were there to work as hard as I was, which was pretty hard.

Mike did the telework thing too until I stopped it.

"You need to be on the premises to keep the division supported and the equipment running, and you can't do that from your house," I said.

He agreed and was okay with it. The administrative support, not so much. For the entire staff in my division in DC, we had one full-time administrative assistant and one part time. That was it. What I discovered was that the lawyers did everything for themselves. How inefficient, but they didn't have a choice. There wasn't administrative staff there to help them.

The full-time administrative assistant decided that her hours were from seven in the morning, before anyone else was there to support, until three-thirty in the afternoon. Although I got to the office by a little after eight each day, most of the other lawyers got there by nine, which was fine. So, this meant that we had administrative support when we didn't need it and no support later in the day when we did.

This was all ridiculous to me, and something had to be done. I actually liked them, but I could tell, given my view of their hours, that it might not have been mutual.

"The administrative assistants can't fill the copiers and escort guests from the lobby to our offices from their houses, and that is a regular part of the job. They need to be here by eight-thirty to five and no telework," I said to Mike.

Oh, what a federal crime I was committing trying to do this. It took months, lots of discussions with human resources, lots of red tape, but I did it. At least my division would have some administrative support.

I was tired at work, still not yet being able to move to the other apartment, and couldn't wait to get a good night's sleep. The work part was going pretty well, though.

The division was coming together and continuing to do great work. We were removing a backlog by reassigning work. Some people had been overworked and others had almost nothing to do. That is kind of how the government runs, but that isn't right. These very talented people deserve a well-functioning place to work.

The people in the division could see that I rolled up my sleeves and worked hard and was a fair person. So, they responded with great support, they worked, and the mood was getting better. It was all coming together, but there was some trouble looming.

There were four commissioners at the Derivatives Trading Commission at the time. The commissioners were appointed by the sitting president of the United States, and there were five slots. Sometimes a position can be open for years. I learned that the government can be inefficient in that way too. And the way these agencies worked, there would be a majority of commissioners from the same party as the sitting president. So there was one Republican and three Democrats. Nobody knew my party affiliation, and they certainly didn't know that my father had been a Democratic alderman in Burbank for thirty-three years until he passed away.

I think that because of my being pro-business, people thought that I was a Republican. Jonathan, the chairman, was a Democrat, and he was the one who hired me. He was a good lawyer. And of course, he hired me, so he had to be smart. We got along, but I didn't feel like he had my back. But I knew he appreciated my technical and management skills.

The Republican commissioner, Gerry Vernon, wrote papers about issues and flew around giving speeches about himself. I couldn't tell whether he was very bright or not.

Once, he put out a statement on a report that my division did. The report was fantastic and very technical. I thought that his statement was negative, self-serving. I thought that it was offensive to the people who worked so hard to put that report out. I thought "what an asshole" and was going to let him know.

I have always believed that as a manager you have an obligation to stand up for your team because they can't, even if it means there are negative consequences to you personally. So, I did. I wrote to Gerry that I thought his comments were disrespectful to the people who worked so hard and that it was not right. I asked that he consider my comments before ever doing something like that again.

We later had a conversation about it, and to Gerry's credit, he said that he had thought about my comments and he could see how what he published could have been taken differently than what he had intended.

"That was not my intent. Do you want me to communicate that to the staff?" he asked.

"I appreciate that, but no. I'll let everyone know that you were sincere."

At that point, I thought he was a stand-up guy. Well, I guess I am not always right.

There was another commissioner, Brad Columbia, who was a Democrat. He was not from the industry, and he and his staff kept asking questions that I thought demonstrated a lack of understanding of the issues. Brad kept saying there are no dumb questions. Well, I think there actually are. I was very nice to them, though, and always tried to be helpful and respectful.

I soon learned that was a one-way street. Brad's most senior staff went behind my back directly to people in my division to ask them questions and even asked them to not tell anyone.

I thought, "What is this, the third grade?"

I went to   Jonathan and said this doesn't cut it. I am running the Division and all work comes through me. That is basic good management. To his credit he did communicate that to the other three commissioners. I heard that Brad was furious.

It was clear to me that although I was helpful and respectful (although with my staff we had a lot of good laughs behind closed doors) it seemed to me that Brad and his staff hated me.

One day I was walking out of the building to get carryout and happened to be with two of my Deputies. One of Brad's staff was rounding the corner with a few people and said distinctly hello distinctly and named my two deputies, with me standing right there. I guess he thought he would show me. I burst out laughing at what was kindergarten behavior.

And then it got more heated. My division had been working on an important industry issue, and we had come up with a good solution to solve the problem. We issued a letter to the industry that found a safe and clever solution. Well, Brad didn't like any of that, so he issued his own statement.

I thought that his statement slammed me and my division and our solution. My staff was very hurt as they worked so hard on this issue and to find the right balance, and they did. And I fully supported them. The truth was that part of the solution was my idea and I didn't want them blamed.

I was furious at the statement that Brad put out in public. I didn't care about myself as I had a thirty-two-year solid reputation and nothing he could do would change that. But I felt bad for my team. These things could be demoralizing, so I decided that he wasn't going to get away with it. It was extremely risky, but I didn't care what happened to me.

I wrote Brad a long email telling him that he was wrong on the substance and disrespectful to my team. I noted that for some in the division, this is their life's work and they are proud of it and I was too. I asked him to consider my comments before doing anything like it again.

Thinking that there was a pretty good chance of getting fired for doing that, I let my deputies in DC know what I had done. I showed them a printout of the email, not wanting it sitting in their email boxes for anyone to think they had anything to do with it. When I showed it to them, they each had a look on their faces of "oh no." They knew there would be fireworks.

I meant it. "If I don't stand up for the people in our division then I don't belong in the lead chair. I'm comfortable with what I've done," I told them.

It was like when I was at Dunkin' Donuts and stood up to the boss who was picking on the shy girl and got fired for it but never regretted it.

I also forwarded the email to Jonathan so he wouldn't be blindsided. He went on vacation, and I didn't hear anything, which was odd.

Oh well, maybe he read it and realized I was right. Well, that's not how it turned out.

When Jonathan got back from vacation, I was called to his office. I was a bit nervous but didn't regret what I had done. He was pleasant and mentioned about the public statement that Brad had put out before he had gone on vacation and asked how was my team doing.

"Oh, we're all fine since I responded to him."

Jonathan seemed confused.

"You responded?" he asked and had a startled look on his face.

"I forwarded the email to you, but maybe you missed it."

"I think I'd better read it," he said.

I left the office not knowing what was going to happen.

Well, about an hour later, I got the call from Beth to immediately go to Jonathan's office. It was like being called to the principal's office. He had his chief of staff with him, and Jonathan's demeanor was different. He was furious and said that Brad was furious too.

"What exactly were you trying to achieve?"

"If you don't stand up for the people who work for you, then you don't belong in the chair," I said.

Jonathan didn't get it that it applied to both of us. That seemed to me to fly right over his head. In the heat of the moment, at least that was amusing to me.

The conversation was escalating quickly, and his chief could see this was not going to have a good ending. He interrupted and the temperature came down slightly. I did what I thought was right and would have done it again. I was prepared for whatever consequences there would be and had started packing up my apartment the week before.

I left his office and let my deputies know what had happened, and they seemed worried as we were all working so well together. And then nothing happened. More days went by, and still nothing happened. And Brad didn't get away with it without being called out.

The division was extremely busy and producing a lot of good quality work. It was clear to me that Brad was going to give me a hard time. At the Derivatives Trading Commission, policy and rule changes happen through the public rulemaking process which is necessary to change a rule. But it takes forever and the other Divisions get to weigh in and drag everything down. It was inefficient, so I used another tool in my box.

A division director can issue what is called a no-action letter, which can come pretty close to achieving what a change to a rule can do. However, it doesn't go through all of the red tape and nonsense, so I had a lot of fun with those. I could achieve so much and do it relatively quickly.

It was amazing the amount of power that I had in this position. There were actually people like me at my level who drove Washington policy and not the guys at the top. I never knew that about Washington and loved that part.

That said, I was very responsible and only issuing positions that would not cause regulatory harm or risk to customer funds. It took my whole career to build my reputation, and I would never risk doing anything irresponsible.

I helped businesses, regulators, universities, and lots of others. Many of the regulations are broken and they never get fixed. That is one of the problems in Washington. It doesn't affect the politicians because they aren't running any productive businesses. That is why I went to Washington to help. And I did.

By the end of my two years there, my team and I had issued more than fifty no-action letters, and Brad couldn't stop me.

CHAPTER THIRTY-TWO

SECRET AGENT MAN

Toward the end of my first year, I got a call from a guy who said he was working on my background check and he needed to do a personal interview. I had totally forgotten about the big background check as it had been so long, and I had written it off at the start as a waste of taxpayer money.

I never understood if he was from the Secret Service or the human resources department of some government entity, and I didn't care. There was just so much red tape. So, he came to the building, and since the administrative staff was now on the premises, rather than at home, they escorted him to my office.

He was nice enough. Keep in mind, this was almost at the end of my one-year merit appointment.

"Why does it take so long?" I asked.

"That's the way it is in the government."

He asked me a few questions but then focused on my dual citizenship. Several years back, I had applied to become a citizen of Ireland. They permitted dual citizenship if you could prove that your parents or grandparents were born in Ireland.

My grandparents, on my mother's side, and my dad's father were Irish immigrants. I was proud of my Irish citizenship and thought I was, in a way, honoring my grandparents and my parents. It took years for my mom to pull together all of the documents to submit as they were difficult to find. Some of the birth records were kept in church basements in Ireland, and some of them no longer existed. My mom, bless her, did all of the work so that I could apply.

When I finally submitted the documents to the Irish Consulate in Chicago, they said it could take a year. They were so lazy. They were only open about four hours a day, so that was no surprise. I finally got my certificate of citizenship and was officially a dual citizen. I also got an Irish passport.

This guy was all over the Irish citizenship thing.

"Why did you get it?"

"Because I could," I said.

"Why do you want it?" he asked.

"Because I do."

He was about to ask another question, and I stopped him cold.

"Look, this means a lot to me—in fact, more than this job, which I don't need. I'm not giving up my Irish citizenship, so you're going to have to find a way to clear it or I'm out of here."

We finished the interview, and I didn't know what was going to happen, but I wasn't giving up my dual citizenship. I didn't belong in this government stuff anyway. At some point, I got something saying I was cleared. I never knew what that meant and didn't care.

CHAPTER THIRTY-THREE

WASHINGTON IS SO COOL

There were so many amazing things about DC, and I was there to take advantage of them. Each weekend, I did something Washingtonish, with the National Gallery of Art being my favorite. I toured the whole thing but appreciated the Impressionist collection the most. The Monets and Renoirs were the best of all to me. They were such treasures and I appreciated them.

I went to the space museum and was so amazed to see all of the real space suits worn by the heroes. I saw the actual United States Constitution in another museum and on another weekend went to Mount Vernon where George Washington lived.

I am a cemetery person, and my parents always have fresh flowers in the summer and fresh wreaths for Christmas. Being a cemetery person, I went to Arlington Cemetery many times. It was so amazing to see that people were from so many different wars were buried there. The history is unbelievable in DC, and I liked seeing the stuff again from when we went on that one family vacation. I was older now and even appreciated it more.

I often went to the Mall on weekends. Not the shopping one, but the official Mall. I would walk from the Metro to the Capitol and then to the Lincoln Memorial and never got tired of it. The war memorials were so well done and honorable. The one that was and still is the most moving to me is the Vietnam Memorial.

It's simple in structure and then you realize what you are looking at. On it is a list of the names of all of the soldiers who served our country in the Vietnam War and were killed. The wall starts out low and proceeds to get higher until it is taller than anyone looking at it, then it gradually reduces in size to the end and the last name.

I cannot walk through it without shedding tears every time. Those soldiers were someone's son, daughter, father, mother, uncle, or aunt, and so many lives were lost. Politicians' names weren't usually included unless they served in a war, only those honorable soldiers who lost their lives serving our country. God bless them for their service and for the biggest sacrifice of all.

One of the most beautiful and uplifting things to do in Washington is to see the cherry blossoms in the spring. Oh, I couldn't get enough of them and I became a blossom junkie. They are stunning, and they don't last for a long time, not even two weeks.

People from all over the world go to see the cherry blossoms. They blossom in the spring and its timing depends on the winter weather and when spring hits. There are pink ones and white ones. Of course, the pinks are my favorite. I did go one weekend in the height of the season and wouldn't do that again. It was wall-to-wall people, too crowded.

Many months later, it was almost time for my first Christmas season in DC. It was kind of depressing as there weren't many decorations. Chicago gets all decked out for Christmas, but not DC.

I mentioned that to my good friend, Kathy, who happened to be Jewish. She said it's because most of the buildings are government buildings, and that they are supposed to have some sort of separation of church and state. I still thought that that was unfortunate; it all looked so gray.

Kathy called. "Hey, I'll pick you up this weekend, and we can go and see the decorations."

"Oh, I'd love to," I said.

I was so glad that she offered and we went to see the Christmas tree on Capitol Hill and the President's Christmas tree. They were puny compared to Chicago Christmas trees and decorations but is was still fun and we had a great day. Back home then in Chicago for Christmas break, I couldn't get enough of the Christmas decorations.

I only had two friends in DC, Kathy and Glenda, and they were and are still great friends. They would call and ask if I needed to get anything and offered to take me to the stores as I didn't have a car. They would also call and ask about doing something on the weekend, lunch or dinner.

I didn't call them often, not wanting them to feel responsible for me. I was so glad when they did call, and we always had fun. But I also spent a lot of time by myself, which was okay, and I got something new from the mall each weekend.

My dear friends Helene and Matt from Melbourne came to visit for a day. They came to the States to visit friends in New York. They took the train so we could spend a day together. I met them at the train station in the afternoon, and our adventure began.

We walked to see all of the museums and the memorials. When we got back to my apartment that night, we couldn't move as we were exhausted. We put our feet in the swimming pool for relief, looking at the Pentagon, and had wine to help with the pain.

The next day, we only had half a day and went to Arlington Cemetery as that is where they wanted to start out. I was amazed that they wanted to see it since they are not from the States and they still wanted to pay their respects. It was touching. We also went to the Vietnam Memorial and they were as moved as I always am when I see it.

They were impressed by everything and so glad to be able to spend time together and to see this stuff. I literally showed them Washington, DC, in twenty-four hours. By the time we walked to Union Station so they could go back to New York, we could barely move or speak. But it was worth it, and I was so glad they came. None of my other friends came, and I wished that they had. Unfortunately, Ryan and Dan never came because with school, the timing never worked.

Things were going along great. The division was working well together and the work was good. And I had a lot of new clothes and shoes from the mall. When the end of my one-year appointment was nearing the finish, the chairman, Jonathan, asked me to stay on for another year. I thought why not. My nephews are in school and DC wasn't nearly as bad as New York was for me. So, I agreed and things continued to progress nicely.

CHAPTER THIRTY-FOUR

SO NOT COOL ANYMORE

And then the U.S. presidential election came and Trump won. Nobody expected that one, and I wasn't sure how I felt about it not being very political. That meant that the Republican commissioner, Gerry, would be the acting chairman and then maybe named by the president to be the permanent commissioner.

The day after the election, I was with my team in Gerry's office making a presentation on an important issue. After we finished, he said, "Would you mind staying back so we can talk?"

He waited until the room cleared before turning to me.

"I'm interested in being appointed by the President to be the chairman of the agency, and I hope that you'll stay on and serve with me. Your work is terrific."

I wasn't sure about Gerry and especially the thought of him being the chairman. But a couple of months later, he was, in fact, was named as the official chairman by the President of the United States.

My team and I met with him and showed him a list of regulatory changes that would improve the industry. He said that he supported all of them and that we should get going on them. That was perfect, as the division was excited to be working on these important changes. We assigned teams and got right to work.

During another meeting with Gerry, he said I was doing everything great and I should keep doing what I was doing. He also complimented me about my management of the division and the great work that we were producing.

Washington and the politics of the Derivatives Trading Commission were wearing on me, and my second year was going to be up in a few months. I had lunch with Gerry, and he again said that I was doing an excellent job.

"I would like to spend more time in Chicago, if that is okay with you."

"That would be fine," he said.

When I got back to the office, his chief of staff, George Benning, whom I thought was an asshole, called me.

"Do you want to move your position permanently to Chicago?" he asked.

I hesitated for a minute, not trusting him, but said yes.

After about a month of red tape, it happened. I was moving back to Chicago where I wanted to be.

The packing was a chore since I had accumulated a lot more clothes. I did find a good charity and they were happy to have any donations, including my bed, which was in good condition. They helped battered women and people in shelters get started in apartments. This was a perfect use of my stuff, and I even gave them my blanket from my family house. Having it brought me such comfort, and since I wasn't going to need it anymore, I wanted someone else in need to have it. It all felt like such good karma.

I had kept those seven boxes from first arriving in DC. They were the ones that did duty as a TV stand, nightstand, and other necessary uses when I didn't have any furniture. I was using those same boxes, and more, to move back.

The FedEx store for shipping the boxes was about six blocks away from my apartment, and I had to get all of them there by myself. I didn't want to impose on Kathy or Glenda, even though they would have been glad to help. I had to make several trips taking two boxes at a time using a borrowed Costco shopping cart. It brought back the bad memories from that move in New York when the moving guy didn't show up and I had to move all by myself in a shopping cart to the other apartment building.

Finally, the last of the seven boxes made it to the FedEx store. I was leaving DC permanently and moving back to Chicago. I was so happy. That day, before going to the airport, my friend Kathy came and we had lunch. I gave her my TV as she said she could use an extra one. She said she would keep it for me in case I wanted to move back to DC. I assured her that it was hers and I was never moving back.

I was so happy to be back in Chicago and could easily do the job from there. The people in the Chicago office were glad to have a division director there, and they were nice to me. It was going well until mid-July when I had a trip to DC and had a meeting with Gerry. Then everything changed.

I had a meeting scheduled with him weeks earlier that he had postponed several times. That seemed off to me, but I didn't think much about it. When I got to Gerry's office, he had his chief of staff with him, and I could tell that the tone in the room was tense.

After some small talk, Gerry finally said, "Your second year is about up, and I'm not going to renew your appointment for another year."

I didn't see that one coming. That was inconsistent with everything he had ever said to me.

What an asshole.

I kept my cool and walked out of the room.

How could Gerry have made all of those statements to me about how great my work was and my management skills and then without any reason given to me do that?

I was angry with myself for not seeing him for what he was. I should have realized that. I thought, well, I didn't want to work with someone like him anyway.

I decided that I didn't want to be one of his swamp rats that he was bringing in. To me, he was just another politician who wasn't going to accomplish much in his role. And, in my opinion, I was right—all bluster and nothing more.

But I didn't have a plan yet. Although the politics in the building was full of backstabbing, and that was the culture with many, it wasn't like that within my division. That was not my tone, and everyone was working together. I thought about it a bit more and decided it was going to be fine and even better. Two years in the government was enough for me.

I finished the last two months of my merit appointment in Chicago, taking a lot of time off as Gerry no longer had my support. And when the two months was over, I knew that I would miss working with the people in my division. I had enjoyed this position, but in the long run, leaving would be better for me and my career. I would miss my team, but I had to keep going.

My parents would have been proud that their daughter made it to DC. I was proud too.

Gerry replaced me with another white guy he knew. There were no women running any division during his time there, despite the fact that there were a lot of talented women in the industry in senior positions and at the Derivatives Trading Commission.

Gerry was so out of touch that, in his official capacity, he even sent a letter to the Pope in Rome about the importance of swaps—which are complex financial instruments. Really? The Pope and swaps? You couldn't make this stuff up. So, I started referring to him as Pope Boy. But I wasn't going to think about Pope Boy anymore. He wasn't worth it to me.

The first week of September 2018, I left that job and remembered that day well as we were closing on the sale of my parent's house the following Monday and had to move everything out the next day. There was too much going on.

CHAPTER THIRTY-FIVE

THE REAL LAST MOVE

I knew this day would be hard, but not this hard. My last day as director ended the day before, but much bigger, we had to move everything out of the house today since we had finally sold the house after having it empty for over nine years. The closing sale was on Monday. My brother and I had kept the house for all this time after my dad passed away. I couldn't part with it, and it was easier to pay the bills every month than to think about selling. I was so emotionally attached to that house and everything it meant to me.

It was our house; we grew up there, and we never lived in any other one. It was the only house my parents ever had. My grandfather had made the down payment and lived there with us until he passed away when I was three and a half. Every memory that I had was, in one way or another, tied to that house in Burbank.

When my mom passed away, my dad had talked about possibly moving because it was so hard on him with all of the memories in the house. At the same time, he couldn't part with those memories and he stayed. I was so glad as it would have broken my heart if he had given up our house. It was never the same for him as my mom was so wonderful and he had never imagined living without her; his heart was broken.

After my dad passed away, I went to the house and did many projects to restore some things to their original condition and paint the inside walls. I thought, surely it would take me years and there was no reason to sell the house while all of these important projects had to be done.

I was honoring my parents every time I was there restoring the house to all of its original glory. And, of course, I would visit the cemetery where my parents were. Remember, I am cemetery gal and all. My parents did so much for me.

We were also so lucky to have the neighbors that we did on our block in Burbank. They looked out for the house during the nine-and-a-half years that we kept it. They were lifelong friends of my parents, and I had known many of them since I was very young.

All the kids on the block grew up together, and many of the parents stayed on the block in their family homes. They were so kind and knew that it was too hard for us to let go of our house. To this day and forever, I have such gratitude to the neighbors on our block.

There were two accidents when I was doing my projects that I will never forget. The first one was in the basement. Of course, I was by myself, standing on a folding chair to reach to the ceiling and move the valve that turned on the water hose on the outside of the house. I probably shouldn't have used a folding chair, but it was the closest thing, and I didn't have any skills to be doing these projects, being a condo gal.

All of a sudden, the chair collapsed and I fell hard to the floor. It was a cement floor with tiles on it. I laid there thinking I must have broken some ribs or something. I didn't have my phone with me since it was upstairs in the kitchen and nobody knew that I was in the basement. I just lay there. After a while, I rolled over and tried to get up. I couldn't believe that I was fine; it could have been bad.

The second accident happened when I decided to trim the bushes in front of the house. I always wanted the house to look nice. But again, I didn't have any skills for this. I found this long-nose electric cutter thing in the garage and it looked like it was used for this type of job. I thought that was what my dad must have used.

I brought it to the front of the house, plugged it in, and started on the project. It was looking good, but the cutter was getting heavy. Without thinking, I took my other hand and reached underneath to lift it up a bit and didn't realize my hand was reaching under the blade. And it happened. It caught my hand.

The cutter stopped and I dropped it screaming, "FUCK!" I was in pain and there was blood all over the place.

The neighbors across the street, Pat and Jim, must have been looking out the window, and they ran out to their porch.

"We saw what happened. Do you want us to call an ambulance?" Jim yelled.

"No, I'll be fine." But I didn't feel fine.

I stood there trying to stop shaking and then looked down at my hand. It sure hurt but the blood had stopped. I was so lucky or maybe someone was watching out for me because this could have been really bad. There was no damage to my hand. It took me a year before I had the nerve to try that project again.

While at the house doing the projects, I never felt alone and always had peace. I was making progress and doing a good job. When each project was completed, it was such a sense of accomplishment, and I knew my parents would like it. I stripped wallpaper, patched walls, and painted the whole inside of the house. That was a big job, but I didn't mind doing it at all.

This went on for years, and I was fine with that. It was too hard to think of letting our house go. When I got the big job in DC, I thought maybe it was time.

"We should think about selling the house since I won't be able to help as much to take care of it," I said to my brother.

We were both sad but agreed we couldn't keep doing this.

"We'll do for sale by owner," my brother said.

"I'm not showing the house to strangers by myself."

"No problem, I'll handle it," he said.

He put a sign in the window and a sign on the front lawn. Both were blocked by the cherry blossom tree, and it wasn't listed on any real-estate listing services. The only way to know that the Flaherty house was for sale was if someone told you. This went on for more than a year, and my brother finally thought it might be time to get a realtor. We didn't want to hold the house going into another winter. We were lucky the pipes never burst, but we knew that this could happen any winter.

One of my projects over the years was to clean out the attic, and it was a big job. When I was young in my room, there was a hole in the ceiling of the closet, and that is how someone would access the attic. I always hated the attic and was afraid of it. I thought someone could be up there when I was sleeping and then jump down and into my room to scare me. I always kept the closet door closed and never went up there.

When my mom was here and I was grown, she had asked me to help her with a project.

"If anything happens to me and your dad, the attic will be a big job for you," she said.

I went there on a Saturday in the winter to kickstart the project. I climbed up the extension ladder and grabbed a few things from the attic and handed them down to my mom, and we were proud of our progress. I didn't have to use the hole in the ceiling in my old bedroom that I was always afraid of since my parents had installed this extension thing in the hallway that folded into the ceiling.

We weren't in any hurry, and I liked working on the project with her that day. The first items were my old ice skates and old skates from the roller rink. They still had the pom poms on them. There was also an old book or two. I took them out to the alley by the garbage for Monday morning pickup, then left and went home.

Later that evening, my mom called to tell me that my dad had gone out to the garbage and retrieved all but the old books. He put them right back in the attic. My mom and I worked on this attic project for two more Saturdays and the same thing happened. He must have not wanted to part with any of our family memories.

My mom and I agreed that we should probably quit the project as most of what I took out to the garbage for pickup, he brought right back in and put it where it was.

"I feel bad for you," she said. "Someday, you'll have to do this by yourself."

I never thought anything about it again until now.

After my dad passed away, I gradually started to clear the attic. It was loaded with stuff, and I could only see what was right in front of me up there. I grabbed what I could that was close to the entry of the extended ladder. Being by myself, I could only bring down what I could carry. It was a slow go, but that was okay since there was no hurry.

There was so much up there. I was so glad that most of it was there, except for old books. Although it was going to take me some time to clear, I was glad that my dad didn't want to part with anything. I was happy now that he kept putting things right back where they were.

The project continued and old stuff was being cleared out of the attic slowly. Then one day, I saw them. As I got closer to the back of the attic, there they were, all of my treasures.

My mom and dad had kept everything that meant something to me as I was growing up, and it was all there in good condition. She knew what I loved as a kid and she kept them all for me, knowing that someday I would find them. All of those years, I wondered what had happened to all my stuff and assumed it had all been thrown out when I moved out after getting a job. It was all there.

It took me back to the moments of each particular item, and I relived the activities and the joy. I brought my Barbie and Ken and Skipper down. They were still in good condition, and all the Barbie dresses too. I even had my plastic Barbie car. And my beautiful little veil from my First Holy Communion Day was there sitting in a box. That was the day when I felt like a princess, and it all came back to me when I opened it.

I couldn't part with any of this stuff, so it is all in my closet except for the veil, which has a prominent place on the dresser in my bedroom. I am glad to be like my dad in that way. The attic that made me so afraid when I was young was now my most treasured part of the house.

There were potential buyers, but it took a while to sell, and then a family wanted to buy our house. I felt that at least our home would go to a family. But I would always think of these people as trespassers living in my house. When I visit the neighbors, it still kills me to see someone else living there.

It will always be the Flaherty house to me. And I was happy to hear that the owners got a ticket for not mowing the lawn often enough. That is the Flaherty house and it has to be taken care of with honor.

The closing was scheduled for Monday morning, so we had to move everything out of the house over the weekend.

"Which moving company are we using?" I asked my brother when we were planning the move.

"We don't need one. We'll do it ourselves."

"There's no way we can move all of this in a day," I protested.

He ignored me.

It was my brother, my nephew Dan, my sister-in-law, and their friend Steve. My sister-in-law did most of the sorting. To make matters worse, the two-and-a-half car garage was filled side to side, front to back, and higher than you could see. It was all my brother's stuff from when he moved from his prior house to his existing house. It all went in the garage.

I will never forget that my sister-in-law brought her dog Charlotte and didn't bring a leash. The dog was a sweet mixed-breed shelter dog. She was so confused that day because she didn't know where she was.

When moving furniture and big items out of a house, the front and back doors had to be open so everything could go out. So, every fifteen minutes or so, someone was screaming for the dog.

"Where is the fucking dog?"

We'd hear it over and over, and there she would be wandering down the street.

There was so much yelling and screaming and swearing that day that our dear neighbors for life steered clear of us. They understood how hard this day was for us, and I think that all of the screaming and swearing was our way of coping with what we were doing.

And there was something very interesting about the dog that day. When she was in the house, we wanted her in the basement, but she wanted no part of that. She wanted to be upstairs and kept going into my mom's room. She would walk to the closet and stare in it. She was agitated and kept going there.

Charlotte went one other place—the front room where my mom used to sit on the couch. She lay there, but she was agitated. They say that animals can sense things that people can't, and maybe she did that day. I knew that my mom would have known how hard this day was on us, and maybe the dog could sense that. I don't know, but there was something.

There was more screaming and yelling, and it was clear that this move wasn't getting done in one day. We would all have to come back the next day and do the rest. I got home and could barely move but went back the next day. But by the time I got there, most of the stuff had been moved out. That tangerine refrigerator from when my parents had their first apartment sadly stayed as we couldn't move it.

"I will stay back to clean," I said when everything else was moved out.

This was my parent's house and the only one we had ever known, and I made sure that it would be handed over in immaculate condition and wouldn't have had it any other way. I also wanted to spend more time there this one last day, and was in no hurry. It was hard to leave because it was sad that someone else would be living there.

I took pictures of each room to always remember them, although I knew every inch of the house. I finally left and said goodbye to our house forever. It was hard driving back to the city as I could barely see through the tears.

The next day, we went to the closing. It was so tense because I didn't want to be there. The family buying the house was speaking in Spanish, so I assumed that they were Hispanic. I was speaking through their lawyer, trying to give them helpful information about the neighborhood and how great it would be for their family.

It came time to hand over the keys, and I was crying.

"Is this your parent's house?" they asked in English.

I couldn't speak and nodded yes. They thanked me for leaving everything so clean and in such good condition.

Then it was over and we left. No more house.

I forgot to mention where everything in the house went. My brother had rented the moving truck, and since we didn't know what to do with everything, it all went straight to his house. We loaded up the truck, and it all got moved to Beverly, his neighborhood. Yep, nothing was thrown out, and it is still there years later. Ryan and Dan joke about wanting pre-death sorting so they aren't left with everything. I am not sure where they came up with that one as it is kind of funny. But it's not going to happen.

A year later, I wanted my mother's hope chest. It had been down in the basement all of those years, and of course, it was at my brother's house. In my mom's day, a gal got a hope chest, which was a cedar wood storage chest, before she got married and stored things in there for when she did. It had been kept in a small heated room in the basement.

At Christmas time, my nephews drove the hope chest to my place. I remember they were so careful with it since it belonged to their grandma, whom they so grateful to have even for such a short time. They were so important to her.

There were some watermarks on the bottom from when the electricity would occasionally go out from a storm, causing the sump pump to stop and some water to get into the basement. It didn't matter to me.

After they left, I opened it to make sure there were no spiders or anything and found that it was airtight. And once again I was amazed. In there were three of my best and favorite dolls, even the Mary Poppins one, all saved in perfectly good condition. I loved those dolls and had assumed, like my other stuff, that they had been thrown out when I moved out of the house. My mom put them in there for me, again, knowing that someday I would find them. And I still have them.

I have been so lucky to have the best parents and our perfect house in Burbank. And I was also so lucky to have traveled so many places in the world and worked with such great people and to have such wonderful friends. While my heart was broken to not have our house anymore, finding these treasures reminded me again of how lucky I had been in life.

Now home for me is where my family is. All of those years of travel, every time counting the days to get back to my family, are over. And I have stayed true to my promise to myself that family comes first.

I am so blessed and filled with gratitude every day.

CHAPTER THIRTY-SIX
STARTING IT AGAIN

The house was gone. It took some getting used to. My job was also over, but my career didn't end there. I wasn't going to let some assholes get me down. I had worked too hard in my life, and they were not worth it.

After doing some thinking and realizing I was always the happiest as a consultant on my own badge as The Global Capital Group Ltd., I decided that was what I should be doing. I knew that it might take a while to get my business up and running again, since it had been shut down for almost six years while I was at my last two jobs. And the two major clients that I had at the time were no longer in existence. They had either been swallowed up in mergers or gone out of business.

But I was up for the challenge and promised myself that I was never going back to work for whackadoos ever again. I would rebuild my business, and do that, no matter how long it took.

When I had my business several years back, it didn't have a website, so I had to figure out how to build one. That was a challenge for me because I had no web design skills. It took about a week to build, and I liked it. It's a simple design, and more of an electronic business card than anything. Marketing is not my strength, so when people asked me what I was doing, I would tell them consulting and let them know the web address. And before long, I was getting requests to do legal and regulatory work for some large and prestigious financial services firms. I couldn't believe that my new plan was actually working again. And it was fun. I had great clients, and they liked my work. And since I was running my own business with no politics, it also gave me great flexibility with my time. I could work whenever I wanted, catching up on evenings and late on the weekends.

CHAPTER THIRTY-SEVEN

A SUPREME

My consulting business was going well, and it was now the end of the last week of March 2019 and I was on a supreme high. It was going to be one of the best weeks of my life. It started on Monday, March 25, 2019, when I left early in the morning and the cab was on time. So far, so good.

This week was so important to me that I didn't want anything to go wrong. And the traffic was light and I had left in plenty of time. Planning well and leaving nothing to chance, I arrived early at O'Hare airport and had three forms of identification in case one got lost. I sailed through the security clearance line and was so glad that so far there was nothing derailing me, although I was nervous because you never know when you travel from Chicago in the winter.

You see, I was going to Washington, DC, to be sworn into the United States Supreme Court Bar on March 26, 2019. It meant so much to me. I was a kid from Burbank (not California), Illinois, and became a lawyer. I made it to the top of the heap in my area of the law, but it was not always an easy sail.

There are other lawyers too that get sworn into the Supreme Court Bar. I am not saying that I am Sandra Day O'Connor or Ruth Bader Ginsberg, who are justices, but to think that someone like me could do this...well, I had never imagined this could happen. And if all went well, it was actually going to happen.

My law school asked a handful of former students if they would be interested in being sponsored to become a member of the Supreme Court Bar on March 26, 2019, and I jumped at the chance. Being admitted to this bar requires sponsors from others who have made it. It is such an honor for a lawyer to be admitted.

For those who don't know much about the United States Supreme Court, it is the highest court in the United States. There are nine justices, each of them has to be approved by the United States Senate, and they serve the position for as long as they want. It is the highest and most honorable position, I think, a lawyer could ever have. They handle important federal cases.

So, back to my trip. We boarded the plane, and there were two, not one, problems. The catering people who put the food and drinks on the plane were late. When they finally got there, I was so relieved. Whew, we could take off now. Then nothing happened. They weren't giving us any information, which always happens on airplanes.

The pilot finally came on the speaker and said there was a technical issue. Oh no. That is the worst message a passenger can get. And for me, being so tense, it was even worse. Technical issue means if they can't figure it out, then the flight will be cancelled.

I kept thinking, "Oh God, please, no. This is too important to me."

It took forever, but a mechanic arrived and was able to fix the problem. Finally, after all the paperwork was done, we left the gate. That was the best feeling. I was going to Washington, DC.

I should also mention that I told everyone that I knew multiple times that I was going to be admitted to the U.S. Supreme Court Bar. I couldn't stop telling people because it was so exciting for me. Then, at some point, not being able to help myself, I thought I should tell strangers too.

Arriving at National Airport in DC, I grabbed the first cab and got to the hotel, which was not far from the Supreme Court. I wanted to be close so if there were no cabs in the morning, I would walk, crawl, or do whatever it took to get there early. When checking in at the hotel, of course, I had to let the people at the reception desk know that I was going to be sworn into the Supreme Court Bar in the morning. Everyone thought it was so cool, and I was on a high.

My law school was hosting a reception at a law firm the night before, for the few of us being admitted from my school, so we could meet each other. Given my good planning, leaving nothing to chance, I had several hours that afternoon before the reception.

I wasn't new to DC, having lived there from 2016 to 2018, and I went on a family vacation in the fifth grade. But I have always been amazed at all that there is in DC and never got tired of seeing it. When I left in 2018, I wasn't anxious to go back. But when this opportunity came around, I had to do it.

That afternoon, I decided to go and see what used to be my favorite sights, but caution, or maybe more like obsessive-compulsiveness, kicked in. I had better go to the Supreme Court building and check everything out and make sure I knew where everything was. Kind of like a dry run.

I was so glad because if I hadn't, the whole thing wouldn't have happened. I checked out the Supreme Court building, all of the areas and the phenomenal history. I was the luckiest gal in the world to be doing this. I found the actual court room where the justices would be sitting and was comfortable now knowing where things were.

I went to the gift shop and went crazy. Everything said Supreme Court on it, so of course I bought everything—mugs, pens, books, and a gavel necklace. After I had bought it all, it hit me that I had to carry all of this around with me for the next few hours.

I decided to come back tomorrow for more. Of course, in the checkout line, I mentioned to several people about being sworn into the Supreme Court Bar the next day. Everyone in the gift shop was talking about it too, and I couldn't help myself.

It was time to leave and make my way to the reception. I was standing outside on the steps of the Supreme Court and asked someone if they wouldn't mind taking a picture of me with my phone. So there I was, the day before being sworn in, standing on the steps of the Supreme Court. I was freezing but had a hard time pulling myself away.

Before leaving the steps, I saw an officer and asked him which entrance to use in the morning, and he showed me the one. There was another man standing next to him.

"You know, men have to wear a suit jacket and women have to wear the equivalent," he said.

"Oh my god, I don't have a suit jacket." I was in a panic.

"They won't let you in," he said.

He clearly saw me about to have a meltdown on the steps of the Supreme Court. He was so nice and helpful and told me to go back in and go to the Clerk's Office and talk to them. I found the Clerk's Office, and thankfully there were two nice gals who worked there.

"The gentleman outside said I had to have a jacket to be sworn in tomorrow and I don't have one," I said. "I brought my best outfit."

I had my beautiful fuchsia blouse, my best Dior silk scarf with pink, orange, and orchid colors from my friend Anne-Marie in Paris. My tights were fuchsia to match the blouse and fancy plum suede loafers. And it was to be topped off with an orchid cashmere pashmina. The skirt was simple black.

I had planned on looking stunning for the justices. I wanted them to notice me and with my color scheme, I was sure it would work. It had taken me all day to pack on Sunday before I left. For some reason, I brought some dark color backups but had no intention of wearing them. I had a black sweater and dark tights, certainly nothing like the fuchsia ones. Certainly, this outfit was not fancy enough for the Supreme Court.

When I described to the two women in the Clerk's Office what I was planning on wearing, their faces went pale.

"You can't wear any of that, and you need to have a suit jacket and it has to be a dark color. "

I was getting upset and ready to cry. "I don't have one."

"There's a clothing store at Union Station, which is the train station, not far away. Maybe they have something, but it has to be dark and conservative."

They were both very nice by letting me know the rules.

I was absolutely panicked and went as quickly as possible to the store. My beautiful outfit would not be seen by the justices, and I would have to be in all dark, drab colors. Luckily again, there was a nice gal who helped me there.

"I need a dark blazer, and it has to be conservative and nothing attractive."

I didn't think this was possible. This was a store for twenty-year-old gals and certainly not where a sixty-year-old woman shops.

We scoured the store and she finally found one, a black double-breasted blazer. It was not something I would ever have worn and never even looked at the price. At the checkout register, I handed my credit card and realized I was going to be sworn into the Supreme Court Bar wearing a thirty-five-dollar blazer. It was probably some flammable fabric too.

Although disappointed that I was not going in my gorgeous outfit, and certainly the justices were not going to notice me in this, I was go grateful that the man had mentioned the dress code to me and that those two women and then the gal in the store helped me. It could have been a disaster. But I got back on my high.

I went on to a reception with the other former law students the night before being sworn in but first stopped for a glass of wine across the street since I was early. Considering myself on vacation and not counting calories, I could have anything I wanted. Before I knew it, everyone at the bar knew that I was going to be sworn into the Supreme Court Bar tomorrow morning. And everyone there was happy for me.

The reception was a nice event to get to know the others who would be sworn in. We were all from different graduating years. Each of them had brought either a spouse or a family member. When asked by the law school a week before the event for the name of my guest, I said that I wasn't bringing anyone and didn't have anyone to bring.

My nephews who are very important in my life were both in college and my brother and sister-in-law work. So, I was there myself and fine with that. The others went to a dinner afterward, but since I had taken such an early flight that morning and was exhausted, I went back to the hotel. I asked the guy at the reception desk if there was a restaurant close by. He pointed me in the direction of two.

Leaving the hotel, I noticed a family of four leaving right in front of me. It was dark and I didn't know this area well, so I walked faster and started a conversation. They were such a nice family. And of course, they then got to know that I was going to be sworn into the Supreme Court Bar in the morning.

I had a quick dinner by myself and headed back to the hotel. I asked the reception guy for a wakeup call and said that someone should come to my room and bang on the door if I didn't answer. I wasn't taking any chances at this point. I also set the alarm in the room and also the alarm on my phone. We were supposed to be at the Supreme Court by eight-fifteen, so I planned on getting there by seven-thirty.

Luckily, all three means to wake up worked. I got ready in my less-than-gorgeous outfit, with my thirty-five-dollar blazer covering everything, and headed out the door. I did bring the orchid-color pashmina as it was freezing out and would take it off when I got there. If they wouldn't let me carry it in, I was prepared to throw my new pashmina away. And I was glad I brought it.

I got to the Supreme Court building at seven-ten, and it was freezing. I asked one of the security police if there was any coffee shop or anything. He said there was one a couple of blocks away. But I didn't want to leave and possibly miss a cue.

So I walked around the building several times. It was just so impressive. The highest court in the country.

Wow.

I must have said that hundreds of times between Monday and Wednesday.

So, at seven-thirty, they opened the gate and I was the first one into the building. And I was comfortable having been there the day before. I was so grateful to have made it into the building.

I went to the cafeteria as someone had said that some of the justices go there to grab breakfast. I was on justice high alert and dying to see even one of them, any one would do.

It was then time to meet up with the other former students from my law school and their spouses. I was the first one there, and then the others started to arrive.

After a while, we were escorted to a private room. I had never seen anything like it. It was so formal and so beautiful with the color scheme based on rich dark green. There were magnificent chandeliers. There were portraits of prior Supreme Court justices who served on the bench before I was even born. There is just so much rich history of the Supreme Court and all of the decisions over the years that have shaped the legal landscape of this country and our daily lives.

We weren't permitted to take any pictures, so I studied it knowing that I would never see it again. We were in the room with a continental breakfast, but I wasn't really hungry. I was too excited and didn't want to spend any time distracted by eating.

Then the door opened and a guy in a strange jacket walked in. Then he was introduced to us as the clerk of the Supreme Court. He is actually The Clerk. He introduced himself, and what a nice guy, he was not full of himself or anything. He explained his formal jacket was part of the court protocol, and it all made sense. He was there to give us instructions on what was going to happen.

I didn't miss a word of what he said and didn't want to make any mistakes. He said that we would be escorted into the court and to our assigned seats. He said that when court would begin, the justices would walk in and then possibly read opinions if they had any. Then the next order of business would be to admit us to the Supreme Court Bar. Each of our names would be called, and we would stand when called. Then we would stay standing to say the oath with our right hand raised.

This was happening.

It was time. We were called to go into the court, and I followed as instructed and made sure I wasn't going in any back row like in the first grade. No more of that for me.

It was so extraordinarily beautiful. There were huge columns. The ceiling wasn't plain; it was richly decorated with panels of flowers outlined in gold. We couldn't take pictures, and in fact, we had to leave our phones in the private room that we would go back to after the court session. I was taking it all in and not missing anything.

When they brought us to our seats, I was shocked. We were so close to the actual bench where the justices hold court. I thought it would be some big auditorium-type setting and that we would be sitting far away. It was even so much better than I ever thought possible. I was sitting probably ten to fifteen feet from where Justice Gorsuch would be sitting.

And then, at a little after ten in the morning, the justices walked in and took their seats. It was unbelievable to actually see the most important lawyers in the country. Their work, through their decisions, has such an important impact with far-reaching and lasting results. I couldn't believe that I was actually looking at the nine justices of the Supreme Court. I was sitting closest to Justice Gorsuch, and he was drop-dead handsome. Each one was so amazing and smart. I was smiling from ear to ear.

They first read two opinions. The first one was read by Justice Elena Kagan, and it was something about whether the states could make rules about federal parks. She read it, and she was brilliant and funny. I didn't think justices could be funny, but they could. Then the next opinion what read by Justice Stephens. He was brilliant too.

And then it was time. The dean from my former law school stood at a podium facing the justices and read a motion for admission. There were two names read before mine, and then he said Eileen Therese Flaherty. I think I jumped out of my chair. Then the other names were read. After all names were read, Chief Justice John Roberts actually did our admission into the U.S. Supreme Court Bar. Another big wow.

We then had to stand to take the oath. At this point, my eyes were streaming tears. I was just so honored and humbled to be there. That someone like me could get to do this was more than I could ever have imagined. I could see some of the justices noticed that I had tears streaming. Maybe they thought that I was some whackadoo because they didn't know my history.

I was the kid from the dummy track who found her way to the law. Nobody, including me, thought a day like this would come for a kid like me from Burbank.

The time came. I raised my right hand and swore to the justices to uphold the honor of the court.

And I always will.

And then we sat down, and the court session began. There were two cases that the justices would hear. They were about gerrymandering, which is about rigging voting districts to control voting outcomes. The first case began, and the lawyer representing the plaintiff was polished and accomplished. His presentation skills and ability to think on his feet were great.

But I was looking at the justices and beaming from ear to ear. And despite my unattractive outfit, I think they did notice me. I made eye contact, or at least I think I did, with every one of them except Ruth Bader Ginsburg. She was a petite woman, and the bench was high I could only see the top of her head.

What impressed me was how engaged the justices were. All except one asked questions. They would each interrupt the presenting lawyer with their question, which revealed how prepared they were. The questions were good, and I was left wondering how would I have answered.

The lawyer was good; he was confident and never seemed to get ruffled as he knew all of the answers. Then it was the defendant's turn, and he was equally impressive. Then each got another turn. I thought I knew how the justices were going to rule in the case, but it would be fascinating to see if I was right.

I couldn't stop staring at the justices. I kept thinking that I was probably not going to get to do this ever again and how it had been my dream to hear oral arguments before the Supreme Court. There was a short break before the second case would be heard. An official announced that anyone who didn't want to stay for the second case could then leave. No way was I leaving.

The second case was about North Carolina, and again the lawyers for the plaintiff and defendant were impressive. But not more impressive than the justices asking the questions and demonstrating how well prepared they were. They showed and I appreciated how seriously they took their job and that they could be witty and funny while doing it.

After the second case, it was time for the justices to adjourn and it was going to be over. Everyone stood and the justices left the room. It was time for us to leave too. I wasn't sad, being so full and satisfied of this experience. It was one I would never forget. When I was leaving, the clerk was standing at his area at the front of the court, and I approached him.

"I want to thank you so much for this."

He was so gracious. "I'm glad that you enjoyed it."

The dean and the former students and I went back to the private room where we started. We had group pictures taken and shared with each other how totally wonderful this had been. It was better than any one of us had thought it could be. There was such a positive energy in the room.

Then we went to the steps of the Supreme Court for pictures. I asked one of the gals to take a picture of me by the column on the top of the stairs.

I am standing on the top step of the United States Supreme Court and have been admitted to the United States Supreme Court Bar.

I went back to the gift shop wanting more souvenirs. I got more of everything but was smart enough this time to pick items that weren't as heavy. I was so full of pride and joy, and this was the best day in my professional life.

Walking from the Supreme Court, I realized I was so hungry and headed toward my favorite café, The Pavilion. It is a simple place by the National Gallery of Art. The day was cool, but it had warmed up and the sun was shining. It was a perfect day.

I ordered lunch, a grilled cheese and a chardonnay since this was a celebration. I found a table, which is not always a given there, and brought my tray over. At a table close by, there was a young guy who looked like a college kid.

When I finished my sandwich, the woman who was collecting the trays asked me if I was finished.

"Go ahead and take the tray, but I'll keep the chardonnay. I'm celebrating."

Of course, I couldn't help telling another person about being admitted to the Supreme Court Bar.

She was such a lovely woman. "What are you was celebrating?"

There I was again telling a stranger, but now it was official. "I was just sworn into the United States Supreme Court Bar."

She knew exactly what it was, and she was so excited for me. We exchanged names. She was Lisa, and we talked for several minutes.

The college kid overheard and asked what it was, and she explained it to him and how big it was. Then he and I started talking. He was a student here from Amsterdam. He reminded me so much of my nephews, so we had a great conversation about school and what he was doing. It was like I was making friends everywhere and the karma was shining.

I went back to the hotel for a break before having dinner to celebrate with my dear friend Kathy. She picked me up, and we went to a casual French restaurant that was so cool. She wanted to hear all about the swearing in and all of the steps before and after. And of course, I was so glad to have another chance to tell it all. I was effervescent about it, and Kathy so enjoyed hearing about it. We had such a nice time, chocolate mousse and all.

Back at the hotel, I decided not to set the alarm and to get up the next day whenever. My flight was at seven o'clock that evening as I thought I might want to go back and see a few sights. I couldn't fall asleep for the longest time even being exhausted. I kept thinking about everything and reliving it.

The next day, I saw all of my favorite sights again and walked for almost five hours. I went from the hotel, which wasn't far from the Capitol, and walked to the Lincoln Memorial, then made my way back, stopping at all the museums and outdoor memorials along the way. It was warm and another bright day. It couldn't have been better.

I went back to the hotel lobby as I had a little time and needed to sit somewhere. The concierge was there, and we struck up a conversation. And yes, you guessed it, somehow the Supreme Court Bar came up. She, too, was happy for me. And then it was time to leave, so I grabbed a cab and saw the Capitol for the last time for now.

I wasn't sure how I would feel about DC on this trip after I worked there from 2016 to 2018, but it was great. DC was shining again, and there were even a few cherry blossoms starting to bloom.

I had overcome many obstacles along the way, starting in the first grade when they thought I was a dummy and then the multiple mergers and job losses and having to keep it going even when I didn't think I could. Now I am doing the best ever.

When I stood on the top step of the United States Supreme Court for the last time that day, taking it all in, I thought my parents would have been proud of me. As I said earlier, when people at the law school asked me whom I would be bringing with me to the swearing in, I said that I would be coming by myself. But I wasn't alone.

It was a supreme event. And I am now a supreme.

About the Author

Photo by Sandro Miller

Ms. Flaherty is the Managing Director of The Global Capital Group Ltd., a regulatory consulting firm and recently completed a two-year merit appointment as a Director at the Commodity Futures Trading Commission. Prior to her public service, Ms. Flaherty was the Global Head of Compliance and Financial Crime Prevention and Americas General Counsel for the Newedge Group. Ms. Flaherty has served as the General Counsel for organizations on Wall Street and in Chicago.